INTERPRETING EARLY INDIA

INTERPRETING EARLY INDIA

ROMILA THAPAR

OXFORD
UNIVERSITY PRESS

OXFORD
UNIVERSITY PRESS

YMCA Library Building, Jai Singh Road, New Delhi 110001

Oxford University Press is a department of the University of Oxford. It furthers the University's objective of excellence in research, scholarship, and education by publishing worldwide in

Oxford New York
Athens Auckland Bangkok Bogota Buenos Aires Calcutta
Cape Town Chennai Dar es Salaam Delhi Florence Hong Kong Istanbul
Karachi Kuala Lumpur Madrid Melbourne Mexico City Mumbai
Nairobi Paris Sao Paolo Singapore Taipei Tokyo Toronto Warsaw

with associated companies in

Berlin Ibadan

First published 1992
Oxford India Paperbacks 1993
Fourth impression 1997
Fifth impression (with corrections)1999

ISBN 019 563342 3

Printed in India at Rekha Printers Pvt. Ltd., New Delhi 110 020
and published by Manzar Khan, Oxford University Press
YMCA Library Building, Jai Singh Road, New Delhi 110 001

Contents

The essays included here were originally published in:

1. K.S. Krishnaswamy *et al.* (eds.), *Society and Change.* Essays in Honour of Sachin Chaudhuri. Oxford University Press, Bombay, 1977. pp. 1–19.
2. *Sociological Theories: race and colonialism*, UNESCO, Paris, 1980. pp. 93–116.
3. *Modern Asian Studies*, 1989, 23, 2, pp. 209–231.
4. *Journal of the Asiatic Society of Bombay*, 1977–78 (new series), 52–53, pp. 365–284.
5. *Proceedings of the Indian History Congress*, Forty-fourth session Burdwan University 1983, Delhi 1984. pp. 3–22.
6. S. Bhattacharya and R. Thapar, (eds.), *Situating Indian History*, Delhi 1986.

Preface

The essays in this collection were, with two exceptions, delivered originally as lectures and later marginally changed for publication. 'Ideology and the Interpretation of Early Indian History', was given at Cornell in 1974; 'Imagined Religious Communities?', was the Kingsley Martin Memorial Lecture at Cambridge in 1988; 'The Contribution of D.D. Kosambi to Indology', was delivered at the Asiatic Society in Bombay in 1980; and 'Early India: an Overview', was the Presidential Address to the Indian History Congress held at Burdwan in 1983.

All these papers, as well as those on Durkheim and Weber, and on the *Itihasa-purana* tradition, are concerned with the historiography and interpretation of facets of early Indian history and society. There is an overlap of themes in some of them and this is almost inevitable in isolated lectures. But this overlap has been retained as it serves to emphasize particular generalizations. The detailed treatment and the juxtaposing of the themes to the analyses of the authors under discussion, do make the treatment somewhat varied. The increasing interest in the historiography of the early period is an indicator of the awareness of the role of ideology in historical interpretation.

ROMILA THAPAR

Abbreviations

ABORI	Annals of the Bhandarkar Oriental Research Institute
CII	Corpus Inscriptionum Indicarum
JAOS	Journal of the American Orientalist Society
JBBRAS	Journal of the Bombay Branch of the Royal Asiatic Society
PAIOC	Proceedings of the All India Orientalists Conference

Ideology and the Interpretation of Early Indian History

It is some times said that the interpretation of the ancient periods of history has little historiographical interest, since they refer to times too distant for an ideological concern to have much meaning for contemporary society, and that the sparseness of the evidence does not provide much margin for ideological debate. This view would not however be valid for the interpretation of early Indian history, where both the colonial experience and nationalism of recent centuries influenced the study, particularly of the early period of history.

In Europe, post-Renaissance interests, which initiated the extensive study of the ancient world, brought to this study the ideological concerns of their own times.[1] These concerns are also reflected in the historiography of India,[2] if not of Asia. The interpretation of Indian history from the eighteenth century onwards relates closely to the world view of European, and particularly British historians, who provided the initial historiographical base.

[1] A. Momigliano discusses some of these in his *Studies in Historiography* (New York, 1966).

[2] C.H. Philips, ed., *Historians of India, Pakistan and Ceylon* (London, 1961), pp. 92–3; Thapar, 'Interpretations of ancient Indian history,' *History and Theory*, 1968, 7(3), pp. 318–35. For a comparative study, see D.G.E. Hall, ed., *Historians of South-East Asia* (London, 1961); Soedjatmoko, ed., *An Introduction to Indonesian Historiography* (Ithaca NY, 1965).

The resulting theories frequently reflected, whether consciously or not, the political and ideological interests of Europe—the history of India becoming one of the means of propagating those interests. Traditional Indian historical writing with its emphasis on historical biographies and chronicles was largely ignored. European writing on Indian history was an attempt to create a fresh historical tradition. The historiographical pattern of the Indian past, which took shape during the colonial period in the eighteenth and nineteenth centuries, was probably similar to the patterns which emerged in the histories of other colonial societies.

Investigation into the Indian past began with the work of the Orientalists or Indologists—mainly European scholars who had made India, and particularly Indian languages, their area of study. The majority of the Indologists, and certainly the great names among them such as Jones, Colebrooke and Wilson, were employed by the East India Company in various administrative capacities. Trained as many of them were in the Classical tradition of Europe, they were also familiar with the recent interest in philology and used the opportunity to acquire an expertise in a new area. As administrators they required a specialized knowledge of traditional Indian law, politics, society and religion, which inevitably led them to the literature in Sanskrit and Persian. Thus, scholarly and administrative interests coalesced.

The nineteenth century saw the development of not only these studies in India, but also the introduction of courses in oriental languages at various European universities and elsewhere.[3] The term Indologist now came to include those who had a purely academic interest in India and who were intellectually curious about India and the Indian past. The study of Sanskrit language and literature not only gave shape to the discipline of comparative philology, but also became the source material for the reconstruction of ancient Indian society. Vedic Sanskrit, the language of the Vedic

[3] J.F. Staal, ed., *A Reader on the Sanskrit Grammarians* (Cambridge, Mass., 1972).

literature in particular, was used extensively in the reconstruction of both Indian and Indo-European society, since the linguistic connection between the two had been established. It was now possible for scholars of Sanskrit to attempt wide-ranging interpretations of what was believed to be the beginnings of Indian history, with little or no personal experience of the Indian reality. One of the most influential of such scholars in his time was Max Müller, whose full and appreciative descriptions of contemporary Indian village communities would hardly have led one to suspect that he had never visited India. Inevitably those who were sympathetic to Indian culture tended to romanticize the ancient Indian past. These interpretations carried the imagery and the preconceptions not only of the sources, but also of those interpreting them.

By far the most influential theory to emerge from Indological studies in the nineteenth century was the Theory of Aryan Race. The word *ārya* which occurs in both the Iranian Avestan and Vedic Sanskrit texts, was given a racial connotation, as referring to the race of the Aryans. They were described as physically different from the indigenous population and their cultural distinctiveness was apparent from the fact that they spoke an Indo-European language. It was held that large numbers of Aryans, described as a branch of the Indo-European race and language group, invaded northern India in the second millennium BC, conquered the indigenous peoples and established the Vedic Aryan culture which became the foundation of Indian culture.

The identification of language and race was seen to be a fallacy even during the lifetime of Müller.[4] Although in his later writings he clarified his views on this identification, it was by then too late, and the idea had taken root. It is curious that Aryan should have

[4] J. Leopold, 'British applications of the Aryan theory of race to India, 1850–70,' *The English Historical Review*, 1974, 89(352), pp. 578–603. For various interpretations of the term *ārya*, see H.W. Bailey, 'Iranian Arya and Daha,' *Transactions of the Philological Society* (London, 1959), pp. 71–91; P. Thieme, *Der Fremdling in Rigveda*, 1938. Who has argued that the term refers to 'foreigner/stranger'.

been interpreted in racial terms since in the texts it refers merely to an honoured person of high status and in the Vedic context, this would be one who spoke Sanskrit and observed caste regulations and rituals. The racial connotation may have been due to the counter-posting of *ārya* with *dāsa*, in the *Ṛg Veda,* and it was argued that the *dāsa* is described as physically dissimilar to the *ārya.*[5] This was interpreted as representing two racial types with the *āryas* evolving later into the three upper castes and the *dāsa* remaining the lowest, included in the *śūdra* caste; the racial identity of each being preserved by forbidding inter-marriage between the castes. The pre-eminence of the *ārya* was explained as due to the successful conquest of the *āryas* over the *dāsas*. The term *varṇa,* etymologically associated with colour and occurring as a technical term referring to the caste organization of society, was used as yet another argument to support the Aryan theory of race. It was believed to provide a 'scientific' explanation for caste, namely, that the four main castes represented major racial groups, whose racial identity was preserved by forbidding inter-marriage and making birth the sole criterion for caste status. The latter half of the nineteenth century in Europe was concerned with the discussion on race in the theories of Gobineau and the growing interest in social evolution. Some of the Indologists were by no means unfamiliar with this debate.[6] The distinction between Aryan and non-Aryan, and the polarity of Aryan and Dravidian suggested by them for the Indian scene, echoes to a degree which can hardly be regarded as coincidental, the Aryan-non-Aryan distinction and the Aryan-Semitic dichotomy based on language and race, in the European context. The suggested social bifurcation is also remarkably similar; the upper castes were the Aryans and the lower castes were the non-Aryans.

The belief in the Indo-European origins of both European and Indian societies intensified the interest in Vedic sources,

[5] *Ṛg Veda* I. 130.8; 1.101.1; 10.65.11.

[6] L. Poliakov, *The Aryan Myth* (New York, 1974).

since these were seen as the earliest survivals of a common past. The village community of Vedic society was looked upon as the rediscovery of the roots of ancient European society. It was described as an idyllic community of gentle and passive people given to meditation and other-worldly thoughts, with an absence of aggression and competition.[7] Possibly some of these scholars, well disposed towards India, were seeking an escape into a utopia distant in time and place, perhaps fleeing from the bewildering changes overtaking them in their own times. Others were defending Indian society from its critics. Eventually the theory of Aryan race gave way to what has come to be called the Aryan Problem, namely, the historical role of the Indo-Aryan speaking people and their identification in early Indian sources.

But the early nineteenth century saw a new direction in the attitude of the administrator-scholars of the East India Company towards Indian history. Some, although they did not romanticize the ancient Indian past were nevertheless sympathetic in their interpretations. Others, in increasing number, became critical of what they called the values of ancient Indian society. This was in part due to the mounting problems of governing a vast colony, with an unfamiliar, if not alien culture. The nature of the relationship between Britain and India was also undergoing change, for trading stations were being substituted by colonial markets. The major intellectual influence, however, was that of English Utilitarian philosophy. James Mill, its first ideologue in the context of Indian history, completed his lengthy *History of British India* in the early decades of the nineteenth century. Mill's *History* claimed to be a critical investigation of the traditional institutions of India. These, by the standards of nineteenth century Utilitarianism, were found to be static, retrogressive and conducive to economic backwardness. He recommended a radical alteration of Indian society, to be achieved by imposing the correct legal and administrative system in India. Both the analysis and the solution suggested by

[7] M. Müller, *India, What Can it Teach Us?* (London, 1883), p. 101ff.

Mill suited the aims and needs of imperial requirements. His *History*, therefore, became a textbook on India at the Haileybury College, where the British officers of the Indian Civil Service were trained.

Further intellectual support for this view of the pre-modern history of India was found in writings of the more eminent philosophers of history of the time. Hegel, for example, remarked on the absence of dialectical change in Indian history, and consequently dismissed Indian civilization as being static, despotic in its orientation, and outside the mainstream of relevant world history.[8]

Central to this view of the pre-modern history of India, and implicit in Mill's *History*, was the theory of Oriental Despotism.[9] The genesis of this theory probably goes back to the Greco-Persian antagonism, with references in Greek writing to the despotic government of the Persians. To this was added the vision of the luxuries of the oriental courts, a vision built partly on the luxury trade with the east from early times, and partly on the fantasy world of oriental courts as described in the accounts of visitors to these regions, such as those of Ktesias at the Persian court and Megasthenes at the Mauryan court in India. The Crusades and the ensuing literature on the Turks of doubtless strengthened the fanciful notion of the all-powerful, despotic, oriental potentate. When interest in the notion was revived in the eighteenth century as an explanation for continuing empires in Asia, the focus was shifted from the doings of the despot to the nature of the despotic state. Given the concerns of eighteenth century France and England, the central question was seen as that of private property in land, and the state ownership of land.[10] Once again, the accounts of ambassadors and

[8] F. Hegel, *Lectures on the Philosophy of History* (London, 1974).

[9] R. Koebner, 'Despot and despotism: Vicissitudes of a political term,' *Journal of the Warburg and Courtauld Institutes*, 1951, 14, pp. 275–80; F. Venturini, 'Oriental despotism,' *Journal of the History of Ideas*, 1963, 24, pp. 133–42.

[10] D. Thorner, 'Marx on India and the Asiatic mode of production,' *Contributions to Indian Sociology*, 1966, 9, p. 33ff.

visitors to Mughal India such as Roe and Bernier were quoted, and they maintained that there was an absence of the right to private property in land.[11] Some, such as Montesquieu, accepted the theory of oriental despotism; others, such as Voltaire, doubted the correctness of its assumptions. By the mid-nineteenth century it had such currency in Britain that again the standard text on the traditional economy of India used at Haileybury College was that of Richard Jones, who endorsed the theory. Inevitably, the major historians of the late nineteenth century in India, who also happened to be the administrators, assumed the correctness of the theory as a precondition to their understanding of the Indian past. Even Marx, despite his concern for dialectical movement, was not averse to the idea with its emphasis on a static society and an absence of change, and worked the theory into his model for Asian society—that of the Asiatic Mode of Production.[12]

The absence of private property in land was central to this model of social and economic structure. The structure was seen in the form of a pyramid, with the king at the apex, and self-sufficient, isolated village communities at the base. The surplus was collected from the cultivators by the bureaucracy, and the process of redistribution led to its being appropriated, substantially, by the king and the court—hence the fabulous wealth of oriental courts. Control over the peasant communities was maintained by the state monopoly of the irrigation system—or the hydraulic machinery, as a more recent author has called it[13]—the control over which was crucial in arid lands dependent on artificial irrigation. The subservience of the peasant communities was ensured not only by extracting the maximum surplus from them, but also by investing the king with absolute powers and divinity. The isolation of social

[11] F. Bernier, *Voyages de F. Bernier . . .* (Amsterdam), 1699. T. Roe, *The Embassy of Sir Thomas Roe to India, 1615–1619* (London, 1926).

[12] R.A.L.H. Gunawardana, 'The analysis of pre-colonial social formations in Asia in the writings of Karl Marx,' *The Indian Historical Review*, 1976, 4.

[13] K. Wittfogel, *Oriental Despotism* (New Haven,1957).

groups was made more complete by the absence of urban centres and effective networks of trade.

The idealization of the village community from one group of scholars was now juxtaposed with the starkness of those supporting the other interpretation. This historical kaleidoscope was readjusted when a third perspective was introduced at the start of the twentieth century. The authors of this were Indian historians, using the current methodology but motivated ideologically by the national movement for independence; scholars who have been referred to in recent writings as the nationalist historians.[14] Of the two major theories, the theory of Aryan race had their approval, whereas that of Oriental Despotism was opposed for obvious reasons. The former was believed to be based on the most up-to-date philogical evidence. Its supposed 'scientific' explanation for caste was gratifying, in view of the general condemnation of caste society from the stalwarts of egalitarianism. *Homo hierarchicus*, if one may borrow the phrase, stood exonerated. The depiction of Aryan society in glowing terms was soothing to the sensitivities of Indian scholarship. There was also an appeal to some middle-class Indians that the coming of the English represented 'a reunion of parted cousins, the descendants of two different families of the ancient Aryan race'.[15]

Nationalist historical writing took up the theme, among other things, of the importance of religion to Indian society. The bipolarity of the spiritual content of Indian culture and the materialist basis of western culture was seen as an essential and inherent difference. This was in part a reaction to the earlier view, that religion was such a central factor in traditional Indian society that it obstructed progress—the latter being defined as social and economic change. This view had been eagerly taken up both by

[14] Such as for example, K.P. Jayaswal, *Hindu Polity* (Calcutta, 1924); R.K. Mookerji, *Harsha* (London, 1926); H.C. Raichaudhury, *The Political History of Ancient India* (Calcutta, 1923), among others.

[15] *Keshab Chunder Sen's Lectures in India* (Calcutta, 1923), p. 323.

Christian missionaries anxious to proselytize among the more enterprising Indian social groups, as well as by those who were looking for a single factor which would explain the backwardness of India as a colonial society.[16]

The nationalist historians concerned themselves with those ideas which were necessary to nationalist polemics. They questioned individual items of historical interpretation, rather than examining the validity of a theory as a total pattern of interpretation. Nor did they attempt to replace the existing theories by new ones, fundamentally different from what had gone before. In a sense, nationalist ideology delimited the nature of their questions. However, in spite of these weaknesses, the impact of the nationalist school was both considerable and necessary. The role of ideology in historical interpretation was recognized with the high-lighting of the ideological content of earlier interpretations. Above all, it prepared the way for questioning the accepted theories.

This has been of necessity an over-simplified sketch of the main ideological trends in modern interpretations of early Indian history. I would now like to consider at greater length the two main theories to which I have referred. In selecting the Aryan problem and Oriental Despotism for further analysis, in the light of new evidence and methods of enquiry, my purpose is not merely to indicate the inapplicability of the theories, but also to suggest the nature of possible generalizations which arise in the re-examination of accepted theories.

The questioning of the Aryan theory is based on the work in recent years from three different disciplines, archaeology, linguistics and social anthropology. The discovery and excavation of the cities of the Indus civilization has pushed back the beginnings of Indian history to the third millennium BC, and the Indus civiliza-

[16] M. Weber, *The Religion of India*, 1958. Glencoe, is the culmination of a range of such views over the nineteenth century. For a discussion of the Christian missionary position, A. Embree, *Charles Grant and the Evangelicals* (London, 1962).

tion has replaced the Vedic Aryan culture as foundational to Indian history. The cities of the Indus pre-date the Vedic culture by at least at millennium, since the decline of the cities dates to the early second millennium and the diffusion of Sanskrit as a part of the Vedic culture is believed to have begun at the end of the same millennium.[17] The Indus cities epitomize a copper-bronze-age urban civilization, based on commerce both within the north-western area of the sub-continent as well as West Asia. The earliest of the Vedic texts, th *Ṛg Veda,* reflects a pastoral, cattle-keeping people unfamiliar with urban life. If the Aryans had conquered north-western India and destroyed the cities, some archaeological evidence of the conquest should have been forthcoming. In only one part of one of the cities is there evidence of what might be interpreted as the aftermath of conquest and even this has been seriously doubted.[18] The decline of the Indus cities is generally attributed to extensive ecological changes. The repeated flooding of the Indus, the rise of the water-table and salination of the land under cultivation, the change in the course of the Sarasvatī river with a consequent encroaching of the desert and major sea-level changes affecting the ports along the west coast, seem more convincing explanations for the decline of the cities.[19] Palaeo-botanical analyses are suggesting a change in climatic conditions from humid to dry.[20] Unlike conquest, ecological change was more

[17] R. and B. Allchin, *The Birth of Indian Civilisation* (Harmondsworth, 1955); R.E.M. Wheeler, *The Indus Civilisation* (Cambridge, 1968).

[18] G.F. Dales, 'New investigations at Mohenjo-daro,' *Archeology*, 1965, 18(2), p. 18.

[19] H.T. Lambrick, 'The Indus flood-plain and the Indus Civilisation,' *Geographical Journal*, 1967, 133(4), pp. 483–95; R.L. Raikes, 'The end of the ancient cities of the Indus,' *American Anthropologist*, 1964, 66(2), pp. 284–99; 'Kalibangan:Death from natural causes,' *Antiquity*, 1965, 39(155), pp. 196–203; 'The Mohenjo-daro floods,' *Antiquity*, 1965; A.V.N. Sarma, 'Decline of Harappan cultures: A relook,' in *K.A.N. Sastri Felicitation Volume* (Madras, 1971).

[20] G. Singh, 'The Indus Valley culture (seen in the context of post-glacial climate and ecological studies in North-West India),' *Archeology and Physical*

gradual and as the cities declined there were migrations out of the cities as well as small groups of squatters moving in from the neighbouring areas. Recent evidence from excavations in western India and the Indo-Gangetic divide is pointing toward some continuity from the Indus civilization into later cultures.[21] There is little doubt now that certain facets of the Indus civilization survived into the second and first millennium cultures, in spite of the decline of the cities. The earlier hiatus between the Indus civilization and the Vedic culture is no longer acceptable, and the Indus civilization has now to be seen as the bedrock of early Indian culture.

Recent linguistic analyses of Vedic Sanskrit have confirmed the presence of non-Aryan elements, especially Proto-Dravidian, both in vocabulary and phonetics.[22] Consequently it has been suggested that Proto-Dravidian could have been the earlier language of northern India, perhaps the language of the Indus civilization, although this awaits the decipherment of the Indus script, and that Vedic Sanskrit as the language of a particular social group, slowly spread across the northern half of the sub-continent, with a possible period of bilingualism, in which Vedic Sanskrit was modified by the indigenous language.[23] It is significant that some of the Proto-Dravidian loan words in Vedic Sanskrit refer to agricultural processes. We know from archaeological evidence that plough agriculture was practised by the Indus settlements[24] and from the *Ṛg Vedic* hymns it is apparent that pas-

---

Anthropology in Oceania, 1971, 6(2), pp. 177–89.

[21] As for example, in the co-existence of the Black-and-Red Ware culture with the late Harappan in western India and that of the Ochre Colour Pottery culture and Painted Grey Ware in the Indo-Gangetic divide and the Gaṅgā-Yamunā Doāb.

[22] A.L. Basham, *The Wonder That Was India* (London, 1954), p. 387; T. Burrow, *The Sanskrit Language* (London, 1965), p. 373ff; M.B. Emeneau, *Collected papers* (Annamalainagar, 1967), pp. 148, 155.

[23] M.B. Emeneau, *Collected papers* (Annamalainagar, 1967).

[24] B.B. Lal, 'Perhaps the earliest ploughed field so far excavated anywhere

toralism and not agriculture was the more prestigious profession among the early Aryan speakers.

Anthropological studies of Indian society have encouraged a reappraisal of the social history of early periods. The insistence on the precise meaning of words relating to social categories in the sources has been all to the good. The valid distinction between *varṇa* as caste in the sense of ritual status, and *jāti* as caste in the sense of actual status is again a help to the social historian. The most useful contribution, however, has been in the study of the formation of castes, which has made it apparent that caste society does not require the pre-condition of different racial entities, nor the conquest of one by the other. It does require the existence of hereditary groups determining marriage relations, which groups are arranged in a hierarchical order and perform services for one another. The hierarchy is dependent on occupation, on certain beliefs of purity and pollution, and on continued settlement in a particular geographical location. The formation of a new caste has therefore to be seen in terms of the historical change in a particular region. Thus, a tribe incorporated into peasant society could be converted into a caste.[25] Occupational groups often acquired a caste identity through the corporate entity of the guild or through hereditary office in administration.[26] Religious sects, frequently protesting against the caste hierarchy, often ended up as castes themselves. Possibilities of social mobility and variations in status were linked to the historical context of time and place. Social attitudes were often set; nevertheless, the opportunities for social change were exploited, and the historian can no longer dismiss the social dimension by merely referring to the unchanging rigidity of

---

in the world,' *Puratattva*, 1970–71, 4, p. 1ff.

[25] N.K. Bose, 'The Hindu method of tribal absorption,' in *Cultural Anthropology and Other Essays* (Calcutta, 1953); D. Mandelbaum, *Society in India* (Berkeley, 1970).

[26] R.S. Sharma, *Changes in Early Medieval India* (New Delhi, 1969) (Devraj Chanana Memorial Lecture.)

caste society. In this context the theory of Sanskritization has been a breakthrough in the study of social history.[27]

The combination of new evidence and fresh perspectives from all these sources raises a host of new questions with reference to the Vedic period. Evidently it was not a purely Indo-Aryan assertion over Indian culture and has to be seen as an amalgam of the Indo-Aryan and the existing culture, which in turn requires a clearer definition of each. Since the spread of Sanskrit, certainly in the Ganges valley if not in the north-west as well, appears to have occurred through a process of diffusion and less through conquest, the motivation for the diffusion would have to be sought. One of the possibilities suggested is that it coincided with the arrival of a new technology at the start of the first millennium BC. This is apparent in the use of iron in preference to copper and the introduction of the horse and the spoked wheel, both new to India.[28] The ambiguity of the word *ayas*, copper or iron in Sanskrit, creates some difficulties in an immediate acceptance of this idea. Vedic Sanskrit is closely connected with priestly groups and the belief in ritual may have accelerated the diffusion, particularly as it seems that Vedic ritual was closely associated with knowledge of the solar calendar providing, among other things, a more effective control over agricultural processes. The diffusion of a language does not require the physical presence of large numbers of native speakers. It can often be done more effectively by influential groups in the population adapting the new language and using the traditional networks of communication. The spread of Sanskrit might be more meaningfully seen as marking a point of social change, apart from merely a change of language.

The notion of historical change, other than changing dynasties, was curiously unacceptable to nineteenth century thinking on the Indian past. The unchanging nature of society is central to the

[27] M.N. Srinivas, *Religion and Society among the Coorgs of South India* (Oxford, 1952).

[28] R. Thapar, 'The study of society in ancient India,' in *Ancient Indian Social History: Some Interpretations* (New Delhi, 1978), pp. 211–39.

theory of Oriental Despotism. The span of Indian history was seen as one long stretch of empire with an occasional change of dynasty. Yet in fact, empires were of short duration and very infrequent. There was only one empire in the early period, the Mauryan empire, lasting from the end of the fourth to the early second century BC, which would even approximately qualify as an imperial system. It was not until the historical writing of the twentieth century that some concession was made to change, and imperial golden ages were interspersed with the dark ages of smaller kingdoms.[29]

In re-examining Oriental Despotism it is not new evidence which provides an alternative analysis, but the more careful questioning of existing sources. It is surprising that references to private property in land should have been overlooked. The socio-legal texts, the *dharmaśāstra*s and the early text on political economy, the *Arthaśāstra*, list and discuss the laws and regulations for the sale, bequest and inheritance of land and other forms of property.[30] More precise information comes from the many inscriptions of the period after AD 500, on stone and on copper-plates, recording the grant of land by either the king or some wealthy individual to a religious beneficiary, or alternatively, by the king to a secular official in lieu of services rendered to the king.[31] These inscriptions were deciphered in the nineteenth century, but read primarily for the data which they contained on chronology and dynasties. In the last few decades, however, they have become the basic source material for the study of the agrarian structure of the first millennium AD.[32] Since these were the legal charters relating to the grants, the transfer of the land is recorded in detail. In areas where the land granted was already under cultivation, the person from whom the land was acquired and the

[29] V. Smith, *The Oxford History of India* (Oxford, 1919).

[30] P.V. Kane, *History of Dharmaśāstra* (Poona, 1942), Vol.3.

[31] e.g. B. Morrison, *Political Centres and Culture Regions in Early Bengal* (Tucson, 1970).

[32] R.S. Sharma, *Indian Feudalism* (Calcutta, 1965).

person to whom the property was transferred are mentioned, together with the location of land, the authority of the officials under whom the transfer was completed and the consent of the village within whose jurisdiction the land lay.

Not only do these inscriptions provide evidence of the categories of ownership of land, but where they refer to waste land it is possible to indicate the gradual extension of the agrarian economy into new areas. This information is of some consequence, not merely to economic history, but also to those concerned with the history of religion; for the extension of the agrarian economy was generally accompanied either by Buddhist missions or by nucleii of *brāhmaṇa* settlements, through which Sanskritic culture was introduced into the new areas and the local culture of these areas was assimilated into the Sanskritic tradition.[33] The interplay of these two levels of belief systems was a necessary process in the delineation of Indian culture. The stress so far has been on the high culture of the Sanskritic tradition which is inadequate for understanding the historical role of cultural forms.

Many of these records provide information on the rise of families of relatively obscure origin to high social status, usually through the channels of land ownership and administrative office.[34] Those who became powerful had genealogies fabricated for themselves, bestowing on the family *kṣatriya* status and, if required, links with royal lineages as well. Such periods of historical change demanded new professions, which professions finally evolved into castes. For example, administrative complexities relating to grants of land on a large scale needed professional scribes. Not surprisingly the pre-eminent caste of scribes, the *kāyastha,* are first referred to in the sources of this period.

The importance given to a centralized bureaucracy in the

[33] This is clearly reflected in the origin myths of ruling families for instance, even in areas as seemingly remote as Chota Nagpur. The origin myth of the Nāgabansis is clearly derived from Purānic sources but also incorporates local mythology.

[34] As for example, the Maitrakas of Vallabhi, during the fifth and sixth centuries AD.

model was perhaps a reflection, among other things, of the nineteenth century faith in the administrator as the pivot of the imperial system. For the bureaucratic system of early India was rarely centralized, except in the infrequent periods of empire. Recruitment was impersonal, and most levels of administration were filled by local people. And it was at the more localized levels that the effective centres of power were located. In periods of empire, the surplus did find its way into the hands of the royal court. But during the many centuries of small kingdoms, the income from revenue was distributed among a large number of elite groups, which in part explains the regional variations and distribution in art styles, where the patron was not a distant emperor but the local king. This tendency towards political decentralization was accentuated from the post-Gupta period *c.* AD 600 when grants of revenue and later grants of land became the mechanism of remuneration.

Bureaucratic control over the economy, such as it was, derived from control over revenue collection. The hydraulic machinery played only a marginal role. Large-scale, state-controlled irrigation was rare. In the main, irrigation aids consisted of wells and tanks, built and maintained either by wealthy land-owners or through the co-operative effort of the village. The more relevant question is not that of the state ownership of the hydraulic machinery, but the variation in irrigation technology and the degree to which irrigation facilities gave an individual or an institution a political edge over others.

The other mechanism of control according to the theory was a belief in the divinity of kingship, which gave the king a religious and psychological authority additional to the political. The attribution of this quality of divinity to kingship was probably the result of earlier studies on kingship and divinity in the ancient Near East. The interrelation between divinity and political authority was never absolute in ancient India. Divinity was easily bestowed, not only on kings, but on a variety of objects, both animate and inanimate. Far from emphasizing divinity, the kings of the Mauryan empire were patrons of the heterodox sects, which denied the existence of any god and ignored the notion of divinity. Divinity was appealed to initially in the rise of monarchy as a political form, in the first millennium BC.[35] But, the maximum references to kings as either incarnations or descendants of the gods coincide with the period of the rise of obscure families to kingship and the fabricated genealogies, suggesting that the appeal to divinity was a form of social validation and its significance was largely that of a metaphor. A particularly subtle aspect of the Indian notion of authority which has not so far received adequate attention has been the interaction of political authority with what may be called the moral authority of the renouncer. Time and again, the renouncer has returned to society and whilst still not fully participating in it, has played a significant role outside the realms of conventional political authority. Whereas political authority (*rājadharma*) derives in part from the power of coercion (*daṇḍa*) and religious authority from ritual and formulae (*yajña, pūjā* and *mantra*), the derivation of the authority of the renouncer is difficult to ascertain, combining as it does elements of the psychological, the social, the moral and the magical.

One of the more striking refutations of an aspect of Oriental Despotism has been that involving the absence of urban centres. The evidence for an early continuous urban economy has been pinpointed by archaeological excavation. This, combined with literary sources, suggests significant variations in the nature of urbanization. That the literary sources were not fully utilized was largely because the details of urban society occur first in the Pāli Buddhist texts, and these were not given the attention which they deserved by those using Sanskrit sources. The cities of the Indus civilization were smaller concentrations of population as compared to those of the second urbanization, linked with iron technology and which evolved in the Ganges valley in the first millennium BC. This had as its economic base trade within the

[35] J. Spellman, *Political Theory of Ancient India* (Oxford, 1964).

sub-continent. The widespread use of coins and other adjuncts to extensive trading relationships, such as letters of credit and promissory notes, not only extended the geographical reach of trade but considerably increased the volume of trade. Steps towards the growth of exchange are apparent in the Buddhist literature relating to the cities of the Ganges valley; but this is less evident in the growth of the cities of maritime south India at the end of the first millennium, where archaeology has corroborated the literary references to a lucrative trade with the Roman empire.

At another level attempts have been made to correlate certain religious movements to the needs of urban groups. The work on the rise and spread of Buddhism and Jainism in relation to the mercantile community has inspired a wider debate on aspects of the *bhakti* movements as being in part the religion of urban groups with elements of dissident thought or, for that matter, the investigation of the Hindu temple as an economic entrepreneur.[36] The outcome of such studies is likely to lead to a rather radical revision of Max Weber's thesis on the social and economic role of religion in India.

In suggesting that these two theories—the Aryan theory and Oriental Despotism—emanating from ideologies pertinent to nineteenth century Europe, are now no longer tenable, it may appear as if I am tilting at windmills. Yet, it is surprising how deeply rooted these theories are, both in India and elsewhere, and how frequently they are revived for reasons of academic study as well as in political polemics. The theory of Aryan race has not only served cultural nationalism in India but continues to serve Hindu revivalism and, inversely, anti-brahmin movements. At the academic level, the insistence on ascribing Indo-European roots to all aspects of Vedic culture has acted as a restraint on the analysis of mythology, religion and cultural symbols from the historical point of view. The intellectual history of a period as rich as that of the

[36] B. Stein, 'Social mobility and medieval South Indian Hindu sects,' *Comparative Studies in Society and History*, 1968, suppl. 3, pp. 78–94.

Upaniṣads and early Buddhism, approximately the mid-first millennium BC, has been hemmed in by the constraints of seeing it in terms of an internal movement among dissident Aryans, rather than from the more meaningful perspective of a period of seminal change. The perennial search for 'the Aryans' continues apace, with archaeologists still attempting to identify a variety of archaeological cultures as Aryan.[37]

Oriental Despotism was revived a few decades ago in Wittfogel's assessment of bureaucratic systems and in association with an oblique critique of the Soviet system. The reincarnation of the theory as the Asiatic Mode of Production has had, I believe, an even fuller transfusion in recent Soviet assessments of the Chinese past, as it has from time to time at the academic level in more general economic analyses of historical change in Asia.

That the interpretation of ancient Indian History was subject to the polemics of political ideology was inevitable. Colonial situations tend to play on the political content of historical interpretation. The sanctity of ancient culture as seen through a nationalist vision made it sensitive to historical analysis. This is not to deny, however, that over the last two centuries, at the level of the discovery of evidence, the scholarship has been both meticulous and extensive. Earlier theories of interpretation have not been replaced as there is now a concern with the need for clearer definitions of historical concepts based on a larger body of precise evidence. This is most apparent in the current debate on the periodization of Indian history. Nevertheless, for a while there was a disinclination to move away from the subject of polemics.

Symbolic of this disinclination was the consistent overlooking of one significant aspect of historical interest: the traditional Indian understanding of its own past. It has long been maintained that the Indians were an a-historical people, since there was no recognizable historical writing from the Indian tradition similar to

[37] e.g. B.B. Lal, 'Excavations at Hastinapura . . . ,' *Ancient India*, 1954–1955, 10 and 11, pp. 5–51.

that from Greece and China. This was in part because the Indian historical tradition — the *iṭihāsa-purāṇa,* as it is called — was in a form not easily recognizable to those familiar with Greek historical writing. Another reason may have been the inability of modern scholars to perceive and concede the awareness of change, so necessary to a sense of history, in the *iṭihāsa-purāṇa,* and this precluded them from seeing the historical basis of the tradition.

The early Indian historical tradition which is now receiving the attention of historians and is being analysed in terms of its ideological content does reflect a distinct image of the past, and its concerns are different from those of modern interpretations of the past.[38] For instance, the unit of history is not the empire but the *janapada,* the territory settled by a tribe, which later evolves into a state, generally a kingdom. References are made to emperors as universal rulers, the *samrāṭ* and the *cakravartin,* but these are at the abstract level. Reality revolves around the kings of smaller kingdoms. The genealogical sections of the tradition explain the settlements of tribes, and with the emergence of states, the association of dynasties.[39] But the past was not recorded as a succession of political events, for the legitimation of political authority was more important and it was to this that the historical tradition gave precedence. The records of these early genealogies were used from the first millennium AD onwards for legitimizing new dynasties who were given links with the ancient royal lineages. Recent work in social history has shown that political power was a relatively open area in early Indian society and the social antecedents of the founders of dynasties were rarely questioned, as long as they complied with the procedures necessary for legitimizing political authority.

[38] Publications on this tradition are F.E. Pargiter, *The Ancient Indian Historical Tradition* (London, 1922); V.S. Pathak, *Ancient Historians of India* (London, 1966); and A.K. Warder, *An Introduction to Indian Historiography* (Bombay, 1972).

[39] R. Thapar, 'Genealogy as a source of social history,' *op.cit.*, 1976, pp. 326–60.

In the Buddhist tradition the unit of history was the Sangha or Buddhist Church and monastic chronicles formed the core of the tradition. These were not merely the history of the Elders of the Saṅgha, for the monastery as an important socio-religious institution played an active political role and its relationship with political authority is apparent from these chronicles.[40]

Cyclic time and the change implicit in the movement of the cycle was the cosmological reflection of the consciousness of change. Even more interesting is the evolution in the form and style of the historical tradition itself, in the latter part of the first millennium AD, when the record includes details of events relating to political authority—in short, the kind of literature which is easily recognizable as historical writing, consisting of biographies of rulers and statesmen and chronicles of dynasties.[41] This new development in the tradition coincides with actual historical change, characterized by small kingdoms generally conforming to the geographically nuclear regions. These were based on a decentralized administration and economic structure, with an extension of patronage to local cultures and the emergence of the devotional religion — the *bhakti* movement—which, through its appeal to a large cross-section of social groups and its use of the regional language, strengthened the regional focus.

Yet the link with the mainstream of the tradition was not broken. Into the early history of the region or the dynasty is woven, quite deliberately, the mythology and lineages of the earlier tradition. The network of Sanskritic culture at least at the upper levels of society was a more real bond between people and places than the mere inclusion of these within the confines of an empire.

The perspective of the ancient Indian historical tradition when seen in juxtaposition with the more recent analyses of early Indian history, apart from its inherent intellectual interest, can suggest

[40] L.S. Perera, 'The Pāli chronicle of Ceylon,' in Philips, ed., *op. cit.*, 1961, p. 29ff.

[41] Such as Bāṇabhaṭṭa's *Harṣacarita,* Bilhaṇa's *Vikramāṅkadevacarita,* Kalhaṇa's *Rājataraṅgiṇī* and various *vaṁśāvalis.*

the ideological concerns of the pre-colonial period. These might provide to the historian of early India a clearer vision of the priorities of the Indian past than have been provided by the polemics of more recent times

*Durkheim and Weber on Theories of Society and Race Relating to Pre-colonial India**

This paper is concerned with the ideas of Durkheim and Weber in relation to pre-colonial India. An attempt is made to examine the colonial comprehension of India, and its influence on these two sociologists—a comprehension which included both early and contemporary India. Such a projection from one historical period onto another was, in many ways, a characteristic of eighteenth and nineteenth century European studies of India. Whatever seemed alien to the European perspective of contemporary India was often visualized as a survival from earlier times and the presumed continuity was imbued with historical authenticity. More frequently the social institutions from the past were believed to persist virtually unchanged into the present and made it legitimate for those studying contemporary Indian society to concern themselves with the texts of earlier periods. Such chronological glissandos were played by both evolutionists and functionalists.

As far as India was concerned, the focus of study was on caste which was seen as the distinctive feature of Indian civilization. This in turn required analyses of Indian religion and the racial

* I am grateful to my colleague Dr Satish Sabarwal for his helpful criticism of an earlier draft of this paper.

composition of the Indian people, since religion and race were seen as essentials of caste. Both Durkheim and Weber tended to concentrate on the former as the more important factor, but this did not preclude a discussion on the latter.

Unlike Weber, Durkheim has written little directly on India. The impact of his thinking is more apparent in the works of his disciples—the sociologists Marcel Mauss, Henri Hubert and Céle-stin Bouglé—and to some extent on a number of Indologists such as G. Held, G. Dumézil and P. Masson-Oursel. Nevertheless, Durkheim occasionally used the existing studies on Indian civil-ization to highlight some of his generalizations. The most often quoted example of this is his argument that religion cannot be defined as a belief in gods since Theravada Buddhism, widely accepted as a religion, did not postulate a belief in gods. Durkheim's concern with the origins of moral and social systems and the dichotomy of the sacred and the profane would have lent itself admirably to an analysis of the interrelations between caste and religion in India, but this clearly was a region with which he felt himself to be unacquainted.[1]

Marcel Mauss and Henri Hubert published a pioneering study on the ritual of sacrifice, *Sacrifice : its nature and function,* in which the Vedic literature with its wealth of detail on the central ritual of Vedic life, the *yajña* (sacrificial ritual) provided the authors with what was until then comparatively new data among sociologists. Earlier studies had centred on Tylor's evidence as discussed in *Primitive Culture* and that of Robertson-Smith's work in *The religion of the Semites*. These studies were based in part on observation (not always of a very systematic kind) with descriptions which were patchy and not nearly as meticulous in detail as were the Vedic texts. Above all, the Vedic texts were sacrificial manuals *per se.* Frazer's attempt to universalize the theories on sacrifice had com-plicated the process of analytical investigation. Hubert and Mauss

[1] E. Durkheim, 'De la definition des phenomenes religieux', *L' année Sociologique*, II (Paris, 1899), pp. 1–28.

were attempting to apply Durkheim's theories to a new area of evidence, a procedure which was to be repeated in some of the essays in the collections published as, *Mélanges d'histoire des religions,* and more specifically by Mauss in *Essai sur de Don.* Subsequently Masson-Oursel in his chapters in the collection entitled *Ancient India and Indian Civilisation* has tried to separate the magical elements from the rational in the structure of early Hinduism and has posed the problem of the expectation of worldly success in the performance of religious rituals. These ideas have been further developed by Heesterman in a study on the ancient Indian sacrificial ritual, *The Ancient Indian Royal Consecration.* Held has used the Durkheimian method more directly in an analysis of the *Mahābhārata* basing himself on a statement from Marcel Mauss, 'Le Māhabhārata est l'histoire d'un gigantesque potlatch'.[2] In *The Mahābhārata: an ethnological study,* Held argues that the Kauravas and the Pāṇḍavas were two phratries and that dicing and war were both part of the symbol of potlatch competitions; that the mythology of the epic revolves around notions of early classifications, such as the constant use of the number five and the cyclic concept of cosmic movement; and that the text distinguishes between the sacred act (*karma*) and sacred knowledge (*jñāna*) particularly in its didactic sections. More recently Dumézil has acknowledged the influence of Durkheim in his studies of Indo-European society and mythology. He argues that all Indo-European societies reflect a three-fold social division (the priest, the warrior and the commoner, what he calls the tripartite function) in the arrangement of their mythologies relating to the deities they worshipped. This in a sense overarches the religious and racial perspective.

Among the nineteenth and early twentieth century analyses of caste in India, Bouglé's work, deriving as it did from Durkheim's ideas of community, religion and stratification, introduced a new dimension and shifted the focus from race and

[2] M. Mauss, *Essai sur le Don* (Paris 1925), p. 143. (trans. *The Gift,* New York 1967).

occupation to new categories of stratification. It is unfortunate that his book *Essays on the Caste System* remained untranslated from the French for half a century; certainly its impact on studies on caste would have had a greater significance. Both Mauss and Bouglé were interested in the Indian data largely because it provided new source material on a society which had not been extensively investigated by sociologists. They were interested in the difference *per se* between Indian society and those with which they were already familiar. Caste society was for Bouglé a contrastive study in a wider area of sociological concern—the study of egalitarianism [3]: a trend which has continued until recent times as is demonstrated by Louis Dumont's *Homo Hierarchicus*.

Weber had a more clearly defined purpose in using the Indian material. He was setting up a model of Indian society in order to prove a series of theses regarding modern European society. The non-European tradition was essential to his analysis not only as a contrastive study but more specifically in order to explain the absence of the emergence of capitalism in areas other than western Europe. His study of Asian religions (India and China) focused on the intermeshing of religion and economic life. Weber was among those who subscribed to the critique of Marx by pointing to what he thought were the inadequacies of Marxist explanation. Capitalism, therefore, was not the result of an historical evolution but a unique development which had its roots in seventeenth-century western Europe. In order to demonstrate his analysis, he had to use contrastive models from traditions other than the European. A precondition to his analysis was the assumption that there were factors in the European situation which made it significantly different from all others and by implication substantially more effective in terms of world history. Weber's interest in the non-European past was not therefore in the essential difference with the European, but in testing and proving a hypothesis concerning the European past.

[3] C. Bouglé, *Essays on the Caste System* (Cambridge, 1971), p. vii. (Originally published 1908 in French).

The choice and comprehension of the Indian material was to some extent conditioned by the use which these sociologists wished to make of it. The reliability and the range of the source material which was available to them by the end of the nineteenth and early twentieth centuries when they were writing is another question which has to be considered. By this time the Indian pre-colonial past had been interpreted by a large number of sophisticated ideologues who, under the guise of the newly-found objectivity of the nineteenth century, were supporting a variety of preconceptions or what they believed were definitive models. In most cases the interpretations were highly coloured by the intellectual preconceptions current in Europe at the time.

The problem of source material operated at two levels. One was that those who were not professional Indologists had to use the sources in translation. This was crucial to the question of interpretation. Terms relating particularly to social organization could only be translated and interpreted in the light of current research. Those for example who were reliable scholars of Sanskrit were not necessarily acquainted with the nuances of social forms and stratification. Consequently, the translation of concepts could result in misunderstandings. For example, the notion of race was embedded in the European intellectual consciousness in the nineteenth century. The universality of the concept was sought to be proved by translating various words as 'race' from the literatures of non-European societies even where the concept of race did not exist. Thus Monier-Williams, an undoubtedly outstanding Sanskritist and the compiler of the standard Sanskrit dictionary, refers to race as lineage and proceeds to translate a series of terms essentially connected with descent groups and kinship relations as 'race'—*vamśa, kula, jāti, gotra, jana, varṇa.*[4] None of these words could today be translated as race. Similarly, the frequently used term, *ñāti*, in the Pāli texts, now often translated as phratry or as

[4] M. Monier-Williams, *A Sanskrit-English Dictionary* (New York, 1976), p. 652.

extended kin-group, was also earlier translated as race. The understanding of caste as described in the *Dharmaśāstra* of Manu would naturally take on a strange coloration if references to *varṇa* and *jāti* were translated as race. This particular example is interlinked with the fact that most nineteenth century theories explaining the origin of caste saw it primarily as a system of demarcating the identities of various racial groups and maintaining separation.

At the other level, the sources of India available to those who were not professional Indologists were generally limited. The primary data on caste was taken from the Census Reports and the Imperial Gazetteers for the contemporary period and from the translations of the *Dharmaśāstras*, the socio-legal texts, for earlier times. The former category was compiled by officials of the Government of India and naturally reflected the conceptual biases then current on the pre-colonial Indian past among British administrators who were also, in the main, the scholars in the field. For the religions of India there were again the translations of the texts and the works of Indologists such as Zimmer, Oldenberg, Fick, Hopkins or historians such as Vincent Smith and Grant Duff.

The investigation of Indian society by European scholars had begun in a systematic way in the late eighteenth century. A major strand in the early interpretations was what became well known in the nineteenth century as the Aryan Theory. It derived academic sanction from the work of comparative philologists such as Max Müller, Auguste Pictet and Christian Lassen, ideological sanction from the essays of the Comte de Gobineau and political sanction by the end of the nineteenth century from the competing imperialism of the West European nations. The basis of the theory was the equation of language with race. In Europe the major dichotomy was seen as between Aryan and Semitic and in India it became Aryan and Dravidian, with the upper castes viewed as the descendants of the Aryans. The association of the theory with India had its genesis in the philological relationships noticed between Sanskrit and Greek, Latin and other European languages.

The Aryans it was argued were implicitly superior to the non-Aryans as they were the initial conquerors who had founded civilizations in Europe and Asia. In India, the arrival of the Aryans was associated with the compilation of the *Ṛg Veda* and this was believed to be the bed-rock of Indian civilization, the excavation of the Indus cities not as yet having taken place. By the late nineteenth century, the fallacy of equating language with race had been clearly demonstrated. Nevertheless, the theory remained established in European thought with reference to India. It also became acceptable to the new middle-class élite in India as it could call itself Aryan, differentiate itself from the lower castes believed to be non-Aryan and even seek a connection with the British rulers who represented European aryandom.[5]

Caste society was explained as being based on racial segregation with the Aryans forming the higher castes. The system was defended as a scientific division of society based on racial grouping, where the identity was preserved by rigid laws of marriage. The linking of caste society with racial segregation grew, in part, out of a linguistic misapprehension. The two most frequently used Sanskrit words referring to caste are *varṇa* and *jāti*. The latter quite clearly refers to descent and derives from the root **ja*—to be born. *Varṇa* on the other hand, which is used to categorize the four groups (*brāhmaṇa, kṣatriya, vaiśya* and *śūdra*), has been derived from a root meaning colour. This was immediately interpreted as a reference to human pigmentation and colour in the racial sense by the early translators of the texts. That the racial connotation is the suggestion of the translators is clear from the entry under *varṇa* in the Monier-Williams dictionary.[6] From the texts it would seem that the connotation of colour is symbolic since the four colours associated with the groups are white, red, yellow and black.[7] Social differentiation symbolized in

[5] *Keshab Chunder Sen's Lectures in India*, p. 323.

[6] M. Monier-Williams, *A Sanskrit-English Dictionary* (New York, 1976), p. 924 qv. *varṇa*.

[7] *Mahābhārata* 12.181.5ff. refers to the four *varṇas* as symbolized by the

colours is not unusual in the traditions of many early societies. Additional support for the racial basis of caste was sought from the references in the *Ṛg Veda* to the initial division of society into the *ārya-varṇa* and the *dāsa-varṇa* wherein the latter is described as being constituted of short-statured and dark-complexioned people, [8] but the description of the former is vague.

Apart from the rather simplistic racial dichotomy, other aspects were introduced gradually as caste came to be seen as the foundation of Indian social structure. Earlier, Max Müller in *Chips from a German Workshop* had argued that the racial factor was not a sufficient explanation for the evolution of caste and had added two more: conquest and political formation and professional or occupational groups. To these, Alfred Lyall had added a fourth, the religious sectarian factor, arguing that religious sectarian movements could also evolve into castes and this evolution was the reflection of the divisive tendencies inherent in Indian society.[9] Ibbetson took the argument further and suggested that three factors were important: the creation of guilds founded on hereditary occupation, the exaltation of the sacerdotal function and the importance attributed to heredity. Caste was consolidated by a series of laws regulating marriage alliances, the purity of food and

---

colours white, red, yellow and black, the differentiaion of which comes about after a preliminary period when all *varṇa*s were identical. The same sequence of colours is used in connection with the four epochs (*yugas*) 3.148.5–37.

[8] *Ṛg Veda* 1.130.8.; 5.29.10.; 9.41.1.

[9] A. Lyall, *Asiatic Studies* (London, 1889); D.C.J. Ibbetson, *Report on the Census of the Punjab taken on 17th February 1881* (Calcutta, 1883); J.C. Nesfield, *Brief View of the Caste System of the North-western Provinces and Oudh, together with an Examination of Names and Figures shown in the Census Report*, 1882. (Allahabad, 1885); H.H. Risley, *The People of India* (London, 1908). These were all officials involved in the administration of India and contributed to the collection of census data and studies of castes and tribes in British India during the late nineteenth and early twentieth centuries. In contrast to the British writing on this subject which came mainly from administrators, French studies on society and religion in India came from professional scholars of Sanskrit and from sociologists.

intercaste relations. The consolidation was largely within the framework of *brāhmaṇa* authority and power. Nesfield argued that occupation was the dominant causative factor. He favoured an evolutionary pattern from tribe to caste where marriage rules and behaviour taboos reflect tribal forms in caste and the occupation taken up by the tribe on the decline of the tribal form identified its caste status. Status was largely determined by whether the occupation was of a pre-metal working society and therefore low or of a post-metal working society and therefore high. The *brāhmana*, however, remained always the highest caste.

Risley revived the race theory in his *The People of India* (1908). He argued that there was a tribal genesis to caste, a memory of which is retained in the exogamous groups such as the *gotras*. But this soon gave way to primarily ethnological distinctions, the germ of which lies in the enemity of the white and black races as expressed in the *ārya-varṇa* and the *dāsa-varṇa* of the *Ṛg Veda*. The segregation was maintained by carefully worked out endogamous laws. He took very literally the Brahmanical idea that all low status castes are necessarily the product of interbreeding. The hierarchy of caste was based on an ethnological distinction between the Aryans retaining their purity as the highest castes and the aboriginal inhabitants of India being clustered at the lower end. Risley maintained that race was the generating principle and he used ethnographic measurement, particularly the nasal index in an attempt to prove his theory.

A rather different point of view was put forward by Senart in his *Les Castes dans l'Inde* (1896). He was dissatisfied with the racial theory. He felt that the emphasis on occupation as the crucial variable was exaggerated since caste distinctions were known even among people in the same profession. Senart sought the answer to the origins of caste in the constitution of the family. Caste has the same rights over individuals as do early families in other ancient societies such as the Greeks and the Romans. Endogamous laws were also fundamental to these societies (e.g. the *jus connubii* of Rome). Laws of commensality in caste were intended to exclude the aliens from sacrifices and religious feasts since a meal signifies sharing and equality. Even the fear of impurity and defilement has analogies from Greco-Roman parallels. The origin of caste requires a multi-causal explanation. He accepted that there was initially a conflict between the Aryans and the dark-skinned race of inferior civilization which resulted in a strengthening of the exclusiveness of the Aryans. Gradually however there was an admixture of races and apart from the extensive family groups which developed into castes, function-based groups of a mixed origin also developed into castes. The sacerdotal power strengthened itself and worked out the ideal caste system—the *varṇa* system. Notions of purity made the exclusion more rigid and prevented absorption into the indigenous population. As in the case of the Greeks, it also preserved the higher castes from performing manual labour. The unending justification of social distinctions was endorsed by the concept of metempsychosis. The continuity of caste was largely due to the absence of a political authority to cut across these divisions and unify them.

The theory of the absence of political authority derived in part from the current notion that the Indian village community contributed to the consolidation of caste since it subsumed common territory, kin and jurisdiction. It was an organic and integral unit which managed to maintain its autonomy from the political superstructure. Max Müller had described it in glowing terms as an idyllic community[10] and it became one of the tenets of nineteenth-century colonial sociology. The village community was also seen as the root of Indo-European life and it was thought that in the Indian village community Europe had rediscovered its origins. Less romantically, Marx argued that the Indian village community was one of the causes of the stagnation of Indian society.[11] Henry Maine saw it as a point along the linear form of the social growth of society from a kin-organized system to a commercial-industrial

[10] M. Müller, *India, What Can It Teach Us?* (London, 1883), pp. 15, 101.
[11] K. Marx and F. Engels, *On Colonialism* (Moscow, 1968), p. 41.

society.[12] Lyall took the argument of an absence of political authority still further and argued that India was at 'an arrested stage of development'. According to him, the evolutionary stage of the tribe was still prevalent (as in parts of Rajasthan) which was a survival from an earlier social form. The absence of political stability was due to an absence of the political institutions required to counterbalance monarchical power.

The notion of Indian society reflecting an early, if not a primitive, stage in social evolution or demonstrating a form of arrested growth was also implicit in another widely-accepted theory which pertained more closely to the nature of political and economic forms in Asia—the theory of Oriental Despotism. Its main postulates were, the existence of isolated, self-sufficient village communities, superimposed upon which was the despotic ruler and his court who creamed the surplus off the peasantry through a very efficient bureaucratic machinery. The latter was not only the mechanism for revenue collection but also ran the State-controlled irrigation system upon which all cultivation was dependent. The divine origin of the king also helped to create the appropriate distance. Since it was believed that there was no private property in land, it was argued that there were no intermediary groups between king and peasant nor, therefore, any political institutions to counterbalance the monarchy. The economic autarchy of the village community allowed it a political autonomy except for the mechanism of revenue collection which impinged on the autonomy. There was also an absence of urban centres specializing in the production of commodities for a market which, had they existed, might have been the basis for a political check on despotism and might have encouraged economic change.

The theory, partially subscribed to by historians such as James Mill in the early nineteenth century, gained ground in England over the decades and by the middle of the century was axiomatic to the understanding of Indian society and politics. Inevitably, it

[12] H.S. Maine, *Village Communities in the East and West* (New York, 1974), (reprint), p. 22ff.

was reflected to a greater or lesser degree in the reports compiled by British administrators working in the districts. Others too were not left untouched. Marx in his discussion on colonialism in India used this theory to explain what he regarded as the political stagnation and economic backwardness of India which facilitated the British conquest. The Indian village community was for Marx a survival from the past and, consequently, an anachronism which had to be done away with if the condition of arrested growth were to cease.

The assumption in these theories was that there is a contrastive difference between the Indian and the European experience. This difference can be explained by locating its causes. The methodological approach was to assume that the Indian experience had failed since Indian society had not evolved to a capitalist form and it was important to try and discover why it had failed. Basic to this assumption was the notion that Indian society reflected a stepping off, as it were, from the escalator of social evolution. This in brief was the intellectual background to the views current in Europe on Indian society. Even where these views were questioned or discarded, the rejection has to be seen in terms of the prevalent ideas. The inability of certain societies to evolve into a capitalist form became a major characteristic in differentiating various societies. This distinction also lay at the centre of sociological thought for many decades and was expressed in a variety of supposed oppositions—*gesellschaft*: *gemeinschaft*, folk: urban, status: contract and, ultimately, tradition: modernity.

Marx had earlier brought to a head the question of the primacy of ideas or social facts. The question arose repeatedly in later writing not only as part of the critique of Marxism but as a controversial issue in itself. Durkheim moved gradually from a position of regarding ideas and beliefs as a derivative of a subsect of social facts towards suggesting that symbolic thought is a condition of and explains society.[13] Durkheim's ideas on the sociology

[13] S. Lukes, *Emile Durkheim: His Life and Work* (London, 1973), p. 235ff.

of religion were important in the analysis of Indian society since religion was often regarded as the crucial variable which gave a particular direction to Indian society, a point of view more fully elaborated by Weber. That the essential elements of religious thought are to be found in seminal form in primitive religion or at any rate, 'it is easier to see the forms at an early stage', is suggestive of an element of evolutionism in Durkheim's argument. There was a tendency to classify religio-social phenomena into two categories: one pertaining to pre-literate societies and the other to literate societies. The Durkheimian interest was essentially in the former with its emphasis on totemism, magic, matrilineal society, the overarching deity and pre-logical thinking, which makes this imperative as a starting point. Religion was pre-eminently a social phenomenon. Although the factual correctness of his use of interrelationships between totem and clan and his reliance on dubious ethnography have been criticized[14] nevertheless his views on religion have been used to correlate religious forms and social realities in Indian society, which have further strengthened the hypothesis of the particular role of religion in Indian society. Since Durkheim's views were largely limited to the religion of primitive societies, their application to Indian data was mainly in the form of recognizing primitive survivals in religious rites and beliefs of the early historical period. Few attempts have been made to apply them to the religious systems of 'tribal India' current even today. The application of his views to more advanced forms of religion in India were limited owing partially to his own initial hesitations in extending his ideas to more complex religious forms.

Durkheim's own analysis did not pertain centrally to Indian religion and even where he uses the absence of deity in Buddhism to point up his definition of religion he is not concerned with any detailed understanding of Buddhism. He argues that the turning in of man upon himself in the process of meditation allows the absence of a deity, a point made by earlier Indologists such as

[14] *Ibid.*, p. 477ff.

Oldenberg and Barth.[15] Nevertheless, Buddhism is a religion since it admits of the existence of sacred things. Buddhism, Jainism and Hinduism enter the discussion again when Durkheim argues that altruistic suicide is a form of sacrifice arising out of a sense of duty and not unrelated to pantheistic beliefs. Durkheim's division of religious phenomena into beliefs and rites reappeared in later studies of the Vedic sacrifice.

Hubert and Mauss analysed the ritual of sacrifice in some detail with frequent reference to the texts on the early Vedic sacrifices. They asserted that the ritual implied the consecration of a common object to a religious plane and that it symbolized the separation of the sacred and the profane. This separation is inherent all the time but can only be actualized through the mediation of religious agents. The separation is apparent at many levels: the area where the sacrifice takes place is demarcated as sacred, the priest communicating with the god is sacred in the sacrificial context as also is the sacrifiant and the mundane animal now consecrated as the sacrificial victim. Outside of a sacred place immolation is murder. As the texts put it, he who performs the sacrifice, 'passes from the world of men into the world of gods'.[16] The preparation for consecration is as elaborate as that of desacralisation. The sacrificer purifies himself by being in a condition of sanctity and redeems himself by substituting the victim in his place. Sacrifice therefore also becomes a procedure of communication between the sacred and the profane worlds. Mauss elsewhere develops the argument with reference to *dāna* (gift giving) which is generally treated as a purely religious action, but he views it as a form of gift-exchange. Using the lengthy discussion on the ritual of *dāna* as stated in the Anuśāsanparvan of the *Mahābhārata* as his data, Mauss argues that a routine action of making a gift can

[15] H. Oldenburg, *The Buddha* (London, 1922), p. 214ff; M. Weber, *The Religion of India* (Glencoe, 1958), p. 146; Quoted in W.S.F. Pickering, *Durkheim on Religion* (Boston, 1975), p. 80ff.

[16] *Śatapatha Brāhmaṇa*, 1.1.1.1ff.

become a sacred rite depending on the donor, the recipient, the place and the intention with which the gift is made, all of which are listed in the text as important factors in the process of *dāna*. Alternatively, the same ritual can be seen as establishing the secular relationships implicit in a gift-exchange.

The bipolarity of the sacred and the profane in the Vedic sacrificial ritual can be seen as embodying social representations in as much as it can be argued that this was also germinal to the idea of purity and pollution with reference to caste groups. The purity of the *brāhmaṇa* was partly derived from his condition of sanctity at the time of the *yajña*, and the exclusion of the other castes may have been measured in terms of their social distance from the sacrificial enclosure. Thus, the *kṣatriya* was frequently the *yajamāna*, he who has the sacrifice performed, and could therefore be admitted as a participant. The other castes were at best observers from a distance.

Clearly, this was but one aspect of caste differentiation and for Bouglé it was by no means the central. Closer to his interest was Durkheim's distinction between mechanical solidarity and organic solidarity underlying which was the notion of pre-industrial and industrial society. The morphological structure of the first which Durkheim characterized as the segmental type—a clan-based society moving to territorial identity—was to be a repeated feature in the discussion on caste. Such societies according to Durkheim, were not based on a division of labour and lacked a fusion of markets and the growth of cities both of which were noticeable in organic solidarity. Other characteristics of the first category were the relatively weak interdependence between the segments, rules with repressive sanctions and the prevalence of penal law and absolute collective authority with little room for individual initiative. Such a society also placed a premium on values relating to society as a whole in its ethical forms, manifested a highly religious conscience and emphasized the transcendental. The transformation from mechanical solidarity to organic solidarity was for Durkheim the central focus of social change with its attendant social integration.[17]

Bouglé examined caste in the light of the definition of mechanical solidarity. He began by investigating whether caste was indigenous to Hindu society alone or was common to all societies at some stage. He includes among the characteristics of caste the following four: hereditary specialization; hierarchy and the inequality of rights; a clear opposition between elementary groups which isolate themselves through a series of taboos relating to food, contact, clothing etc., and which resist unification; and the incidence of mobility being collective rather than individual. When considering the roots of the system, Bouglé disagrees with the explanation that the *brāhmaṇa*s were the originators of caste using it to divide and control society which he felt laid too great an emphasis on religion. The theories of some Indologists who saw caste evolving out of industrial guilds and therefore gave prominence to hereditary specialization were also unacceptable to Bouglé, for this would require an equation of caste with economic function and occupation, and such an equation is thwarted by a series of overlapping relations in caste. Senart had listed three groups among the *ārya*s: the sacerdotal who had appropriated the sacrificial ritual, the aristocracy founding itself on heredity, and the common people. These three divisions provided the impetus for further divisions and the separation of the Arya from the non-Arya. Senart was looking at the origins of caste with reference to *varṇa*. For Bouglé the protypes of caste were not the *varṇa*s but the *jāti*s which were lineage descendants and indicated the dominance of ancient familial exclusivism. Such exclusivism was not specifically Aryan; tribal societies are known to have had rigid rules of exogamy and commensality and fraternity taboos are also to be found among the Semites.

The pre-eminent status of the *brāhmaṇa* was not secured from

[17] It has been suggested that Durkheim understated the degree of interdependence and reciprocity in mechanical solidarity and overstated the role of repressive law. Lukes, *op.cit*, p. 159ff.

the start, but was gradually usurped by the *brāhmaṇa* after an initial competition for status between the *brāhmaṇa* and the *kṣatriya*. Bouglé argued that since the *brāhmaṇa* caste could not accumulate riches its essential strength lay in religious power which it exploited and in this was encouraged by an absence of political organization. The prestige of the *brāhmaṇa* arose out of many factors. The racial superiority of the Aryans who conquered the Dravidians was partly responsible since the *brāhmaṇa*s salvaged what they could of their Aryan inheritance by careful marriage regulations. However, he qualified this by stating that it could not be based on physical types but on the perception of differences among ethnic groups. In addition, the *brāhmaṇa*s had become the guardians of the sacrifice and as such were in a perpetually consecrated condition (a view rather similar to Hubert and Mauss) which was reiterated by an emphasis on avoiding pollution through food and touch, all of which strengthened the exclusivity of the *brāhmaṇa*.

Caste therefore resulted from a concurrence of spontaneous and collective tendencies subject for the most part to the influence of ancient religious practices. The closed cult of the first familial groups prevented castes from mingling and the respect for the mysterious effects of sacrifice finally subordinated them to the castes of priests. The ideas which generated the caste system argued Bouglé, are not peculiar to the Hindus or to the Aryans, but were the common patrimony of primitive peoples. They survived in India because they managed to resist the influence of any unifying forces cutting across the exclusive groups. Thus, Hindu civilization is characterized by an arrested social development. Indian society has moved in an inverse direction and has continued to divide, specialize and hierarchize whereas other societies have unified, mobilized and levelled. Thus, caste society had the same roots and origins as egalitarian societies, but unlike the latter, which underwent changes in the egalitarian direction, caste society deliberately remained inegalitarian.

The lack of social and historical change is specifically noted by Bouglé who uses this as a partial explanation as to why there are neither historians nor historical records in pre-colonial India. He maintains that superficially political forms have changed and there have been administrative monarchies and feudal politics, but beneath this the caste structure has preserved a constant form. Even religion does not succeed in destroying caste since religious sects take on the characteristic identities of castes. The only exception to this was Buddhism and significantly Buddhism did not survive in India. Its disappearance was not due to Hindu intolerance, since intolerance requires political dogmatism which was lacking in India. Rather it was the abstracting of the Buddhist community from social life which prevented it from denting the caste system and furthermore the monastery was closed to those in opposition to authority. Philosophies of detachment and inaction are not conducive to change and the theory of transmigration encourages neither reform nor revolt nor change.

On the question of race Bouglé did not totally discard racial identities in caste although he was unsympathetic to the theories of Risley and anthropometry arguing that castes are not pure races and are racially mixed. To correlate caste and race in accordance with Brahmanical theory (of course assuming that this *was* in fact Brahmanical theory) is to superimpose the theory on observed data. Further, hereditary specialization has not deposited essentially different properties in different castes, as was occasionally suggested by other commentators on Indian society. Bouglé was of the view that the philosophy of race remains unproven, although castes as strictly enclosed groups may have preserved primitive repulsions of a racial nature.

In his discussion on law and caste Bouglé appears to have relied heavily on Durkheim's description of mechanical solidarity. Bouglé maintains that rules relating to behaviour are governed by notions of purity and are therefore largely ritual prescriptions. Unlike western law which is restitutive, the *dharmaśāstra*s of India in which the laws are coded, are repressive. The legal system did not seek to cut across caste distinctions and instead supported the hierarchy of castes and the stress on inequality by assuming an ascending scale of punishment. Hindu law was able to preserve its religious colouring because no political power arose to counterbalance the power of the priestly caste nor did economic life change caste. Caste did not obstruct economic production—if anything it assisted in perfecting the dexterity of the craftsman based on hereditary specialization and the intensive practice of skills. But caste did obstruct economic change in that it retained the primitive clan character of society and mechanical solidarity could not give way to organic solidarity. In the terminology of Henry Maine, status repels contract. Since caste is essentially divisive and separatist, economic groups could not arise which would cut across caste boundaries and the organization of authority left little place for the institutions of liberty. There was never a body of towns large enough and numerous enough for the production and circulation of wealth and at the same time the production and circulation of ideas acting as the necessary centres of co-ordination. Centres of production were associated with political capitals and were therefore transitory. Commerce was never predominant in law, action and style. The city requires a unity among citizens to safeguard its independence, but this was inimical to caste. Guilds were rooted in caste since they could not adopt new members or associate socially among themselves. Thus, there was an arrested development of economic formations, a generalization on which Weber was to expand.

Some of Bouglé's views on India are shared by Weber. His focus was not on caste however but on the absence of the emergence of capitalism. European capitalism was seen as the watershed or the divide separating pre-capitalist from capitalist societies and the dichotomy was emphasized by many theorists at the time such as Tönnies, Simmel and Maine.[18] Marx saw it as a stage in historical development, but Weber saw it as a totality, as a 'civilization'. Central to this totality was the role of rationality in western capitalism which made it a unique experience in world

[18] S. Hughes, *Consciousness and Society* (New York, 1961).

history.[19] This was not to deny the rationality of other civilizations but to point to the generally more static role of rationality in these as compared to its dominant role in western capitalism. Weber tended to pose rationality and irrationality as bipolarities which are present in every situation. Rationality permeated the whole of capitalist culture. It dominated science, law (a written constitution regulating political activity), music, architecture and above all economics, where it is evident not only in the more obvious technological basis of industrialization, but also in the separation of industrial from household economics and the precise analysis of cost and profit which lies at the core of capitalist enterprise. All these in turn tend to impersonalize relationships and conduct (and perhaps even dehumanize certain segments of society). In addition to rationality, there was also the historical factor of the simultaneous emergence of free labour without any land and the industrialist who had accumulated capital through the mercantile activities of the pre-capitalist world.[20] This was a major element in the rise of capitalism which Weber conceded to the Marxist model. The third factor which Weber stressed was the Protestant religion which he felt embodied the spirit of capitalism. Weber's emphasis was on the role of Protestantism in developing capitalism rather than on Protestantism reflecting the rise of capitalism.[21] Weber did not accept the possibility of establishing laws of social development and thereby predicting social change as had been proposed explicitly by Marx and suggested implicitly by Durkheim. He rejected evolutionary theories and maintained that the best analysis was based on categories and 'ideal-types'. The social scientist was also not in a position to make a representation of reality. Methodology was merely a means of understanding—hence the exaggeration implicit in his 'ideal type' was deliberate in order to highlight differences and clarify the model.

[19] J. Freund, *The Sociology of Max Weber* (London, 1968), p. 5ff.

[20] J. Lewis, *Max Weber and Value-Free Sociology* (London, 1975), p. 67.

[21] R.H. Tawney, *Religion and the Rise of Capitalism* (Harmondsworth, 1961), pp. 89–142.

Weber's explanation for the absence of capitalism in India required a detailed examination of religion in India, the two being intertwined. But, apart from examining the religions of Asia, he also argued for certain historical situations in Europe having provided some base for the growth of capitalism. His attempt to locate the latter was by discussing the absence of capitalism in antiquity. It was from this perspective that he viewed the historical development of the pre-capitalist world, both the agrarian structures of ancient civilizations and the rise of the medieval city.

Weber's discussion on the absence of capitalism in antiquity appears to be somewhat anachronistic and arises no doubt from his refusal to make concessions to alternate forms of historical evolution. Yet at the same time he does speak of stages in the social organization of agricultural societies. These he describes as the walled settlements of household and village, the fortress, the aristocratic city-state, the authoritarian liturgical state, the hoplite polis and the democratic citizen polis.[22] The initial stage was characterized by a distinction between free members and slaves and the emergence from among the former of princely clans, their justification being based on division of spoils, voluntary gifts and special allotments of land enhanced by divine legitimacy. The second stage sees the emergence of the king and greater dependence on rent from land. The aristocratic city-state emphasized the status of those who owned land and debt slaves (often peasants who could not pay rents). The feudal nobility of the fortress stage became the urban community, although Weber does not explain the emergence of either. The fifth stage refers to the power of the state and its imposition of duties on the subject. The hoplite polis, a derivative of the aristocratic polis, was subject to the domination of the clan and was characterized by a self-equipped citizen army dependent on ownership of land. This, in turn, gave way to the final stage of the democratic citizen polis where land ownership

[22] M. Weber, *The Agrarian Sociology of Ancient Civilisations* (London, 1976), p. 69ff.

was closely regulated but at the same time separated from military service. Communal forms of land ownership were abolished and rent alone remained. This led to the rise of capitalism since slaves were not debt slaves but purchased. Sharecroppers and slave agriculture gave way to yeomanry and mercenary armies replaced the hoplites. Ultimately city-states declined and were replaced by monarchical state systems with their major structural unit in the manor, channelling land relations, taxes and military recruitment. Weber saw the large empires of Asia such as the Assyrian and the Persian as conglomerates of urban and manorial areas. Yet at the same time he accepted the theory of the absence of private ownership of land in Asian civilization. He argues that, whereas in Europe the pattern of settlement moved from cattle breeding to agriculture and private ownership of land emerged on the basis of communal grazing grounds, in Asia it changed from nomadism to horticulture and the notion of private ownership was thus by-passed.[23]

Weber argues against the possibility of a capitalist economy emerging in the ancient past because the cities were centres of consumption rather than production. The urban economy of cities was limited since they were dependent on grain imports, their export articles were based on high labour inputs which required the purchase of slaves and their policies were solely determined by commercial interests. The development of capitalism was not based on rent from land but on commodity production. Slave agriculture could be regarded as capitalist although here Weber would be subjected to the same criticism as that made of Rostovtzeff's views on capitalist agriculture in Greco-Roman antiquity.[24]

[23] *Ibid.*, p. 37ff. Horticulture implies a mixture of food-gathering and primitive food production requiring neither technological innovations nor substantial changes in demographic structure and land-rights as were necessary in the transition from cattle breeding to agriculture.

[24] M. Reinhold, 'Historian of the classic world: a critique of Rostovtzeff,' *Science and Society*, 1946, 10, pp. 361–91.

In his study *The City*, with particular emphasis on the medieval city, Weber moves away from earlier theorists who had emphasized religion, legal structure replacing kinship, contract replacing status and economic institutions providing the theoretical basis of the city. Weber argues that it is the evolution of the urban community as an institution which characterizes the basis of the city. Above all that the urban community is typical of Occidental society and is virtually absent in the Orient (except in the ancient Near East). It is based on the dominance of trade-commercial relations and characterized by the presence of fortifications, a market, a court reflecting partially autonomous law, association of city members with partial autonomy and administration by authorities in whose election the burghers participate. With reference to India, Weber argued that only guilds and castes developed courts and special legal structures but even here trial by law and courts were absent. Autonomous administration was virtually unknown. The Indian urban dweller remained a member of the caste, guild or city-ward, but not a citizen of the city. There was no joint association representing the city and this was prevented by the segregating necessities of the system. Endogamous castes with their exclusive taboos were an obstacle to the fusion of the city dwellers into a status group enjoying social and legal equality and the ban on commensality among castes prevented the display of solidarity and fraternity of those sharing a common table. The only exceptions to this were that in periods of salvation religions, guilds could sometimes cut across town loyalties if they subscribed to the religion; and in the periods prior to the rise of bureaucratic kingdoms there were autonomous cities governed by clan elders. Indian cities were essentially royal centres or political capitals with market places and fortifications.

Medieval Occidental cities (and especially those north of the Alps) were strikingly different from Asian cities. They grew as a result of immigration so that local ties were eroded and the city became an administrative district within which all inhabitants irrespective of differences shared the same administration. Taboo barriers of totem, caste and clan were absent. On the contrary, the *conjuratio*, the oath-bound fraternity of burghers, broke through some of the earlier tendencies towards separation. Weber's rather glowing account of the medieval Occidental city tends to blur the distinctions within the citizens where both fraternity and autonomy tended to belong to limited groups. For Weber, the most important aspect of the city, namely civic development, emerged neither in the Asian city nor in the medieval European city. It emerged later in the West European city. He gives among possible reasons for its absence the lack of city fraternization which encourages the growth of the urban community. Clans and castes were mutually exclusive. There were no urban military interests and the burgher was not a military man. The guilds in the cities of India and China could bring pressure on royal power, but could not oppose it in a military manner. In the later European cities the guilds could not only combine and assert civic power, but the *conjurationes* could take up arms independently of the king. It was this ability to unite as citizens, demonstrate independence and defy royal power which made the difference. The legalization of privileges encouraged political autonomy. In Weberian terms traditional domination gradually gave way to legal domination. The occurrence of a charismatic figure was not precluded, but the potential for a reciprocal relationship so necessary to the theory of domination would be reduced in a society built on legal domination and the bureaucracy.

Charismatic leadership was more apparent in the role of the prophet in early societies.[25] Here Weber differentiates between the exemplary and the ethical prophet. The Buddha typifies the first where there is no divine mission, the prophet merely showing his followers the path to salvation. Moses as an ethical prophet highlights the claim to communion with God and demands obedience as an ethical duty. The exemplary prophet is common in India and

[25] *The Sociology of Religion* (London, 1965), p. 46ff.

China because of the absence of a personal transcendental and ethical god and also because the rationally regulated world had its point of origin in the ceremonial order of sacrifice. The difference between Asia and Europe is spotlighted by another fundamental notion, that of predestination. In Europe predestination strengthened the idea of vocation and gave the Christian a justification for his activity as being ordained. Success was a sign of God's blessing. Whereas in Asia it provided a negative impulse where salvation lay not in vocation but in escape from the sufferings of the terrestrial world. Similarly, there were basic differences in the nature of asceticism. Christianity culminated in asceticism of the inner-worldly category not the contemplative withdrawal of the world-rejecting type in Asia. Man had to ethically justify himself before the Christian God and not submerge himself. Christian monasteries placed a premium on labour and work rather than on meditation and the bureaucracy of the Christian church required an involvement in life. Some of these contrasts filled out the dichotomy which Weber was posing between Europe and Asia, a dichotomy which he analysed at greater length in his detailed studies of religion in China and India.

It is evident from looking at the sources which Weber consulted in writing *The Religion of India* that he was influenced by the current theories of nineteenth century Indologists and historians, relying as he had to on secondary works.[26] Weber's analysis of the social structure of India was a background to his understanding of both the orthodox doctrines of Hinduism and the heterodox doctrines of Buddhism together with the influence of popular religion on these. Caste and religious beliefs were therefore linked and, ultimately, he was concerned with the impact of religious beliefs on the secular ethic of Indian society. Weber sees caste as a status group with rigid rules of intermarriage and social intercourse and with pollution acting as a discriminatory factor between castes.

[26] *Ibid.*, p. 344ff.

According to Weber, the spread of caste society was brought about by three agencies: conquest, the conversion of tribes into castes, and the sub-division of castes. As a result of conquest racial differences led to segregation and prevented intermarriages, although Weber did not believe that racial differences were inherited. Whereas for Weber race was not the basis of caste as Risley had argued, the juxtaposition of racial differences were significant for the development of caste in India. The conquerors claimed rights in land and the conquered became subservient and lost their rights. Weber makes much of the difference between what he calls 'guest' and 'pariah' people without realizing than many 'guest' peoples were not given the lowest status in caste as he assumes. The conversion of tribes into castes was a commonly held theory among the ethnographers of the time. Tribes and castes had a totally opposite structure and the gradual conversion began with the assimilation of ruling groups among tribal societies into Hindu society generally by their being given *kṣatriya* status.[27] It was also said that food-gathering tribes who had lost their land as a result of the expansion of the agrarian economy were sometimes assimilated *en masse* as a single caste, usually that of peasants. The sub-division of castes meant that a new caste could branch off from an existing one by migration, a change in ritual duties, entry into a new religious sect, inequality of property possession where the better-off would imitate high caste social norms or a change of occupation arising out of economic or technological change. A difference of caste was established with the denial of connubium and commensalism by the original caste and the renunciation of ritual duties by the new caste.

Weber argued that the formation of castes was fundamental to the Indian social order which is based on clan charisma. Even feudal state formation did not rest on land grants but derived from

[27] E.W. Hopkins, 'The social and military position of the ruling caste in ancient India as represented in the Sanskrit epics,' *Journal of the American Oriental Society*, 1899, 13, p. 57ff.

sib, clan, phratry and tribe. The historical evidence however indicates that it was the making of land grants from the first millennium AD that broke the clan charisma. This evidence was available to Weber in the translations of epigraphical data but he, like the historians of the time evidently overlooked this. In the absence of genuine feudalization he argued that there was a prebendalization of the patrimonial state.

The *śūdras* as craftsmen he described as helots of single villages receiving a fixed wage or artisans in self-governing villages selling their products directly or through traders, or artisans settled by the kings, the temple, the landlord and, whether bondsmen or free, subject to servitude, or, finally, independent artisans settled in well-defined parts of the city and working as wage earners. For the *vaiśyas* the caste of traders and merchants, Weber drew his information from the description given by Baden-Powell, and maintained that they could not struggle against the patrimonial prince because of the caste system as well as the pacifism preached by the salvation religions. The stress on pacifism degraded the status of the peasant and inhibited the traders from creating an urban militia. Caste had a negative effect on the economy since it was anti-rational and traditionalistic. Ritual laws stood in the way of economic and technical revolutions. The trader remained a merchant incapable of using a new form of labour power and of diverting his wealth into capitalist forms. Neither was there any chance of cross-caste associations leading to the autonomy of the city nor was there any fraternization of castes as in European guilds followed by the seizing of political power. Caste emphasized distance rather than association. Cities were fortresses rather than urban centres with a weak market nucleus.

Enveloping the social totality was the theory of *samsāra* and *karma* (transmigration and rebirth) which developed into a system for the first time in Buddhist thought. Although Buddhism denied the existence of the soul and merely postulated the continuity of consciousness through a cycle of rebirths, it nevertheless related the ethics of rebirth to caste and this became axiomatic to both

Hindu and Buddhist social philosophy. *Karma* transformed the world into a strictly rational, ethically determined cosmos representing the most consistent theodicy ever produced in history. But it also required the strict fulfilment of caste obligation. Ethnic and economic factors were no doubt significant to caste structure, but *karma* reinforced it at the ethical level. There was no universally valid ethic but a compartmentalization of private and social ethic with each caste having its own ethic and, therefore, men were forever unequal. The absence of ethical universalism led to striving for individual salvation based on attempts to escape the wheel of rebirth. Even asceticism was a striving for personal, holy status where gnosis and ecstasy were sublimated to personal salvation as also were the natural sciences. Rational methods of asceticism were directed towards irrational goals. Yogic and ascetic techniques had two purposes: they had to accommodate the holy through the emptying of consciousness and they sought gnostic knowledge through meditation and techniques conducive to meditation. The salvation doctrines within which Weber included Buddhism, Jainism and the Bhāgavat-*bhakti* aspects of Hinduism, showed scant interest in the ethic for life on a temporal plane. For them reality consisted of the eternal order of the universe and the rebirth of souls.

Weber described Buddhism as the polar opposite of Islam and Confucianism: it was an unpolitical and anti-political status religion of wandering and intellectually schooled mendicants. It was a salvation religion—an ethical movement without cult or deity and centred on the personal salvation of the single individual. Above all, it advocated that the will to life has to be destroyed in order to achieve *nirvāṇa*. Although Buddhism did have a levelling, democratic character, it nevertheless did not attempt any rational method in life-conduct. Weber explains the schisms in Buddhism from the fourth century BC onwards as being due to a lack of strong roots in society, its marginal demands on the laity and its essentially monastic and itinerant way of life. When the monks became materialist minded and accepted gifts and proselytized, the religion declined. This decline was helped by the antagonism of secular rulers to Buddhist monasteries and the rising power of the town guilds. The Brahmanical restoration as Weber saw it continued to emphasize irrational ends. Ritualistic activities were strengthened because the *brāhmaṇas* wished to protect their fees and prebends. Instead of a drive towards the rational accumulation of capital, Hinduism created irrational accumulation chances for magicians, mystagogues and the ritually oriented strata. Brahmanism was supported by rent from land and fees for religious services which were inheritable and given in perpetuity. This encouraged a bifurcation of religious and secular authority and led to the weakening of the latter. In addition, local autonomy was strengthened as against a centralized system. The absence of a secular ethic was particularly apparent from an equal absence of the characteristics of European Protestantism. There was no devotion to a calling in Calvinistic terms with its attendant economic success nor could a rational transformation of the world be postulated as an act of Divine Will. The other-worldliness of Indian religion did not diminish an interest in this world, but the aim of this interest was different. Therefore, even if people were materialistic by nature, they were influenced by non-materialistic ideology into channelling their materialism to ineffective ends.

Perhaps the most frequently used word in Weber's analysis of the religion of India is 'absence'—reflecting a sharp distinction in his mind between the characteristic features of the Occidental civilization and their absence in the Asiatic/Oriental. To this extent he was echoing a common belief among nineteenth-century European thinkers for whom the dichotomy between Occidental and Oriental was very real. This was enhanced by the supposed duality between materialist and spiritualist civilizations, a duality which was to play an even more dominant role in the ideology of Asian nationalism in the twentieth century. The stress laid by Weber on the rationality of developments in Europe came under attack and such analyses were seen as part of a larger racial framework in which ideologues other than Weber attached value judgements of *a priori* superiority to the rationality. This was of course quite apart from the question of whether rationality was the prime motive in the development of European capitalism, a question which has been legitimately raised by some of those examining the place of Weber's thought within the European ideological tradition.[28]

Weber's understanding of capitalism has its own limitations. He fails to distinguish between the two major phases of capitalism—merchant capitalism and industrial capitalism. Thus, the characteristics of the first tend to get extended into the second. Hence the stress on the Protestant ethic, which undoubtedly was significant in the crystallization of the first phase but of only marginal significance to the second phase. What was central to the second phase was colonialism; both in its early form resulting from the colonization of Latin America and industrialization in the second phase dependent on the colonization of Asia and Africa. The ploughing in of the profits of colonialism into the development of European capitalism made a qualitative difference to the nature of capitalism. This not only accelerated industrialization but provided to capitalism precisely the kind of momentum which made it of consequence to world history and more than just a localized European phenomenon. Had the latter been the case, sociological theory in nineteenth-century Europe would not have regarded capitalism as the great divide in the classification of societies. Up to a point this reflects the inadequacies of the understanding of the process of industrialization and capitalism current in Europe at the time. Weber's ideal-type draws on the second phase, but he seeks to explain it by reference to the characteristics of the first phase. The uniqueness of western capitalism became apparent to him when the consequences of the second phase were being felt in Europe. The advance of Europe against the arrested growth of Asia was an established postulate in European thought in the nineteenth century. It was the nature of colonialism which

[28] S. Hughes, *op. cit.*, p. 330ff.

was seen as the historical manifestation of the advance. The initial inadequacy of Weber's theory is the absence of any reference to the role of colonies in the development of capitalism. Even if seen as a unique civilization, Weber's analysis of capitalism was restricted to its nascent phase and to that extent it was incomplete. His dismal prognostications for the future as envisaged in bureaucratic systems, tended to jump from the nascent to the mature without adequately examining the intervening phases.

It is doubtless Weber's refusal to concede historical evolution which led him to inquire into the possibility of capitalist forms in antiquity, both European and Asian. His historical probings would have been more apposite had he analysed non-European history during periods immediately prior to the rise of capitalism in Europe. This he was probably prevented from doing as he did not visualize historical change in Asian societies. Weber was clearly influenced by the concept of Oriental Despotism and, although he does not elaborate on this point, he saw Indian society basically as a static society. Whereas he does see at least three faces to the form of Modern Europe in Judaism, Greco-Roman antiquity and medieval Europe, in the case of India and China, he views them almost as faceless monoliths. This leads to his underplaying even though aware of it, the change within religious movements or social groups as, for example, his repeated references to Buddhist monks as itinerant mendicants even for periods when some were well-settled property owners. This weakness also relates to the discrepancy in the source material which he consulted for Europe and India. In the former case his generalizations are based on data recorded by the actual groups under discussion but in the Indian case he uses the media of Brahmanical texts for virtually all his major generalizations.

Weber accepts the primacy of religion above all other facets in Indian society. This is perhaps what prevented him from examining the more clearly-defined economic aspects at the root of capitalism in his study of Indian society. Whereas the availability of free labour and the existence of accumulated capital is a prior requisite for the emergence of capitalism, he nowhere attempts to assess the availability of these in India. To this extent Weber subscribed to the current lack of interest in the economic institutions of Indian society. Indian civilization was defined as Hindu and Buddhist with a sprinkling of Jainism. Yet it was precisely in the period of what has recently been called incipient capitalism in India, i.e. the seventeenth and eighteenth centuries, that the Islamic ethic, both religious and political was an important factor. A study of merchant capitalism in India would have involved the need to look at Islam in India, particularly at communities such as the Bohras and Khojas of Guajarat and the west coast, of for that matter even non-Islamic communities such as the Parsis. The exclusion of Islam stemmed from the nineteenth-century tendency to identify religions with their areas of origin and therefore Islam was limited to West Asia. To search for the roots of capitalism in the religious ethic of India during the first millennium BC and the first millennium AD is, to say the least, an anachronistic exercise.

Weber's study of India was a by-product of his main thesis and it would be unfair to be too critical of his theories, particularly as he was relying on secondary material for data. It is strange, though, that he should not at any point have questioned the contextual bias of his sources. One can only assume that his faith in the rationality of contemporary scholarship was as axiomatic to him as his faith in the rationality of capitalism. One cannot criticize him for the limitations of his source material but only for accepting unquestioningly the current interpretations and for not applying his own methodology to these sources—an accusation which can equally well be levelled at Marx in his writings on Asia.

In their analyses of caste both Bouglé and Weber were basing themselves on the existing theories without questioning too closely the premises of these. That the argument was often circular did not seem to matter too much, as for instance, in the Census Reports where the model of caste often related to the Brahmanical *Dharmaśāstras*. It has however to be remembered that they were writing over half a century ago with no access to the more recent insights into the social and economic history of India. Early models without the advantage of detailed research tended to result in over-simplification. Thus, in spite of arguing quite correctly that caste formation often took the form of the conversion of a tribe into a caste, there was all the same an acceptance in Weber's writing of the racially distinct character of upper and lower castes.

Caste is seen as divisive and separatist, but it can be maintained that at another level it is associative and this is expressed for example in the uniformity of certain cultural patterns over extensive geographical areas. This aspect is not analysed. The horizontal perspective played a significant role in the spread of 'Hindu civilization' at the élite levels, and was crucial to the extension of caste society. It was again the associative character of caste which was fundamental to major social and economic changes from the late first millennium AD onwards, particularly in periods of state formation. It could be argued that the nature of caste underwent a fundamental historical change during this period—a change which has not been fully recognized by historians and sociologists.[29] So strong was the preconception of the unchanging character of Indian society that generalizations based on the sources of the Vedic period (1000 BC) were considered adequate for the pre-colonial period up to the eighteenth century AD. For example, the status of the *brāhmaṇa* is rightly linked with his control over the sacrificial ritual in the Vedic period. However, with the extensive granting of property to the *brāhmaṇa* in livestock, in gold and ultimately in land there was a qualitative change in the status of the *brāhmaṇa* by the end of the first millennium AD as also in the sacrificial ritual. Far from abstracting a community from social life, the monasteries (the Buddhist *vihāras* and the Hindu *maṭhas*) were also to take on the role of social institutions with substantial political and economic functions. These institutions became parallel seats of power. Alienation from society would have been one reason for joining the monastery but ac-

[29] Romila Thapar, *The Past and Prejudice* (New Delhi, 1975).

celerated social and political mobility could as well have been another. The renouncer rapidly acquired both social status and charisma and frequently built on it a worldly ambition. The 'this-worldly' role of the renouncer seems to have been missed by these sociologists.

From the monastic centres, both Hindu and Buddhist in their time and later even Islamic, there arose the foci of sectarian and political orthodoxy as well as heterodoxy and opposition which led them into varying relationships vis-à-vis political authority. Such religious centres often doubled for networks of trade and were therefore in close contact with merchants and guilds. The nature of the relationship between guilds and political authority was earlier believed to be one of subservience from the former towards the latter, but this view requires re-examination with the availability of more specific and local source material relating to the seventeenth and eighteenth centuries. The jockeying for power between political authority and merchant interests in India during this period suggests a more complex relationship than had been supposed earlier. The crucial question may remain the same as the one posed by Weber, namely, the inability (real or seeming) of the merchants to make an open bid for political power. The answers to such questions lie perhaps less with caste as the crucial variable and more with the role of the European trading companies in Asia. It is curious that Weber did not examine the sources for this period in detail. Had he done so his analysis may have been sharper. But perhaps this would have required of Weber too great an emphasis on historical perception.

From the perspective of the limitation of source materials perhaps the greatest injustice is done to the analysis of Buddhism. Theravada Buddhist sources composed in Pāli were generally regarded by Indologists as somehow not as reliable as Brahmanical, Sanskrit sources. The former were assumed to be *parti pris* but strangely enough not the latter. Since Buddhism had died out in India, Buddhist texts were not given the same importance even though at the time of their composition or soon after, Buddhism was as important, if not more so, as Brahmanism. Had Weber looked more fully at Buddhist sources he would have seen a different epistomology with an emphasis on the universal ethic within which the caste structure was adjusted (and not just the absence of the former and an insistence only on the caste ethic), a movement in time from a pristine utopia to a well-defined future, a strong sense of sectarian historiography impinging on political history of a more secular nature and a monastic life deeply embedded in a society of lay-followers. The three major characteristics as defined by Weber seem doubtful since Buddhism was often closely associated with political authority, at the level of popular support it assimilated local cults and far from advocating a destruction of the will to life it endorsed a programme for the householder and lay-followers which precluded monasticism. Many of the sectarian splits within Buddhism arose because of its having to adjust to changing social mores as it spread across India and Asia. The decline of Buddhism in India had more to do with the changing role of the monastery as an institution, together with competition from other religious sects and a decline in patronage with the decrease of trade in the middle of the first millennium AD.

Weber makes a distinction between early Buddhism, a religion of salvation-striving monks and the later phase with the emergence of what he calls monastic landlordism. The salvation-striving monks were from the start part of a monastic order and the monasteries were segments of what might be called parallel societies. The development of monastic landlordism is seen by Weber essentially in terms of change within the Buddhist structure and to a lesser degree as the interplay between Buddhist institutions and the other institutions of society. Monastic landlordism tends to take on a static form which does not conform to the historical evidence; nor is the emergence of monastic landlordism merely the result of extensive support from the laity since the nature of the institution was such that it made demands both on political authority and the economy. When, even the forest-dwelling monks, theoretically seeking isolation were willing to accept royal patronage and become the nuclei of political centres, the role of such monasteries takes on various political dimensions.

It is not the intention of this paper to attempt to refute the interpretations of Bouglé (as linked to Durkheim) and Weber. Both studies have been seminal to much that is new and meaningful in the sociology and social history of India. A more serious concern with the validity of these interpretations would undoubtedly result in still newer areas of research and analysis. Its intent was to suggest that both Bouglé and Weber in their studies on India were influenced by the prevailing preconceptions about India, which preconceptions they surprisingly tended to accept without too much questioning. One wishes that Weber had applied some of his more innovative categories of thought to the pre-colonial Indian past as he did to the European past.

ADDITIONAL BIBLIOGRAPHY

Baden-Powell, B.H., *The Indian Village Community*, New Haven, 1957 (originally published in 1896)

Bendix, R., *Max Weber, An Intellectual Portrait*, London, 1960.

Dumezil, G., *Mythe et Epopée*, I and II, Paris, 1968, 1971.

Dumont, L., *Homo Hierarchicus: The Caste System and Its Implications*, New York, 1972.

Durkheim, E., *The Division of Labour in Society*, New York, 1964 (reprint and trans).

——, *Primitive Classification*, Chicago, 1963 (reprint and trans).

——, *The Elementary Forms of Religious Life : A Study in Religious Sociology*, London, 1915 (reprint and trans).

Heesterman, J.C., *The Ancient Indian Royal Consecration*, The Hague, 1957.

Held, G.J., *The Mahabharata : An Ethnological Study*, London, 1935.

Hubert H., and M. Mauss, *Sacrifice : Its Nature and Function*, London, 1964 (reprint and trans).

——, *Melanges d'histoire des Religions*, Paris, 1909.

Mill, J., *History of British India*, London, 1818–1823.

M. Müller, *Chips from a German Workshop,* I and II, London 1867–75.

D. Kantowsky has edited of papers entitled, *Recent Research on Max Weber's studies of Hinduism,* London 1986, in which he argues that many scholars working on Weber's theories on India have misunderstood Weber because the translation of his study on the religion of India has misrepresented the original German text. This may well be. One expects therefore a more correct translation to be made available. A recent study which touches on many aspects of this essay is T. Trantmann's *Aryans and British India* which demonstrates the "twinning" as he Calls it of Sanskrit studies and ethnology in the nineteenth century understanding of early India.

*Imagined Religious Communities? Ancient History and the Modern Search for a Hindu Identity**

My choice of subject for this lecture arose from what I think might have been a matter of some interest to Kingsley Martin; as also from my own concern that the interplay between the past and contemporary times requires a continuing dialogue between historians working on these periods. Such a dialogue is perhaps more pertinent to post-colonial societies where the colonial experience changed the framework of the comprehension of the past from what had existed earlier: a disjuncture which is of more than mere historiographical interest. And where political ideologies appropriate this comprehension and seek justification from the pre-colonial past, there, the historian's comment on this process is called for.

Among the more visible strands in the political ideology of contemporary India is the growth and acceptance of what are called communal ideologies. 'Communal', as many in this audience are aware, in the Indian context has a specific meaning and primarily perceives Indian society as constituted of a number of

* I would like to thank K.N. Panikkar, Neeladri Bhattacharya and B.K. Matilal for their helpful criticism of an earlier draft of this lecture.

religious communities. Communalism in the Indian sense therefore is a consciousness which draws on a supposed religious identity and uses this as the basis for a political and social ideology. It then demands political allegiance to a religious community and supports a programme of political action designed to further the interests of that religious community. Such an ideology is of recent origin but uses history to justify the notion that the community (as defined in recent history) and therefore the communal identity, have existed since the early past. Because the identity is linked to religion, it can lead to the redefinition of the particular religion, more so in the case of one as amorphous as Hinduism.

Such identity tends to iron out diversity and insists on conformity, for it is only through a uniform acceptance of the religion that it can best be used for political ends. The attempt is always to draw in as many people as possible since numbers enhance the power of the communal group and are crucial in a mechanical view of democracy. This political effort requires a domination over other groups and where the numbers are substantially larger, there is a deliberate emphasis both on superiority and the notion of majority, a notion which presupposes the existence of various 'minority communities'. In the construction of what have been called 'imagined communities',[1] in this case identified by religion, there is an implied rejection of the applicability of other types of divisions in society, such as status or class.

In the multiplicity of communalisms prevalent in India today, the major one obviously is Hindu communalism since it involves the largest numbers and asserts itself as the dominant group. I shall therefore discuss only the notion of the Hindu community and not those of other religions. Nevertheless my comments on communal ideology and its use of history would apply to other groups claiming a similar ideology. I would like to look at those constituents of Hindu communal ideology which claim legitimacy from the past, namely, that there has always been a well-defined

[1] B. Anderson, *Imagined Communities* (Vaso, 1983).

and historically evolved religion which we now call Hinduism and an equally clearly defined Hindu community. Implicit in this are the historical implications of Hindu communalism and I shall argue that it is in part a modern search for an imagined Hindu identity from the past, a search which has drawn on the historiography of the last two centuries. The historical justification is far from being the sole reason for the growth of communalism, but recourse to this justification fosters the communal ideology.

The modern description of Hinduism has been largely that of a *brāhmaṇa*-dominated religion which gathered to itself in a somewhat paternalistic pattern a variety of sects drawing on a range of Buddhists, Jainas, Vaiṣṇavas, Śaivas and Śāktas. The texts and the tradition were viewed as inspirational, initially orally preserved, with multiple manifestations of deities, priests but no church, a plurality of doctrines with a seeming absence of controversies and all this somehow integrated into a single religious fabric. Differences with the Semitic religions were recognized and were seen as the absence of a prophet, of a revealed book regarded as sacred, of a monotheistic God, of ecclesiastical organization, of theological debates on orthodoxy and heresy and, even more important, the absence of conversion. But somehow the logic of these differences was not built into the construction of the history of the religion. Hinduism was projected largely in terms of its philosophical ideas, iconology and rituals. It is ironic in some ways that these multiple religious sects were seldom viewed in their social and historical context even though this was crucial to their understanding. Histories of the 'Hindu' religion have been largely limited to placing texts and ideas in a chronological perspective with few attempts at relating these to the social history of the time. Scholarship also tended to ignore the significance of the popular manifestation of religion in contrast to the textual, a neglect which was remedied by some anthropological research, although frequently the textual imprint is more visible even in such studies.

The picture which emerges of the indigenous view of religion from historical sources of the early period is rather different. The prevalent religious groups referred to are two, Brahmanism and Śramanism with a clear distinction between them. They are organizationally separate, had different sets of beliefs and rituals and often disagreed on social norms. That this distinction was recognized is evident from the edicts of the Mauryan king Aśoka[2] as well as by those who visited India and left accounts of what they had observed, as, for example, Megasthenes;[3] the Chinese Buddhist pilgrims Fa Hsien and Hsüan Tsang;[4] and Alberuni.[5] The Buddhist visitors write mainly of matters pertaining to Buddhism and refer to the *brāhmaṇa*s as heretics. Patañjali the grammarian refers to the hostility between Brahmanism and Sramanism as innate as is that between the snake and the mongoose.[6] Sometimes the *brāhmaṇa*s and the *śramaṇa*s are addressed jointly as in Buddhist texts and the Aśokan edicts. Here they are being projected as a category distinct from the common people. Such a bunching together relates to a similarity of concerns suggestive of a common framework of discourse but does not detract from the fundamental differences between the two systems. It might in fact be a worthwhile exercise to reconstruct Brahmanism from the references to it in Sramanic and other non-Brahmanical sources.

A historical view of early Indian religion would endorse this dichotomy and its continuity even in changed forms. Early Brahmanism demarcates the twice-born upper castes from the rest. The twice-born has to observe the precepts of *śruti*—the *Vedas* and of *smṛti*—the auxiliary texts to the *Vedas* and particularly the *Dharmaśāstras*. *Dharma* lay in conforming to the separate social observances and ritual functions of each caste. The actual nature

[2] J. Bloch, *Les Inscriptions d'Asoka* (Paris, 1950), pp. 97, 99, 112.

[3] J.W. McCrindle, *Ancient India as Described by Megasthenes and Arrian* (London, 1877); Arrian, *Indica*, XI.I to XII.9; Strabo XV 1.39–41, 46–9.

[4] J. Legge, *Fa-hien's Record of Buddhistic Kingdoms* (Oxford, 1886); S. Beal, *Si-yu-ki:Buddhist Records of the Western World* (London, 1884).

[5] E.C. Sachau (trans. and ed.), *Alberuni's India* (Delhi, 1964 reprint), p. 21.

[6] S.D. Joshi, ed., *Patañjali Vyākaraṇa Mahābhāsya* (Poona, 1968), II. 4.9; I. 476.

of belief in deity was left ambiguous and theism was not a requirement. The focus of worship was the sacrificial ritual. Brahmanism came closest to having a subcontinental identity largely through its ritual functions and the use of a common language, Sanskrit, even though it was prevalent among only a smaller section of people.

Śramanism, a term covering a variety of Buddhist, Jaina, Ājīvika and other sects, denied the fundamentals of Brahmanism such as Vedic *śruti* and *smṛti*. It was also opposed to the sacrificial ritual both on account of the beliefs incorporated in the ritual as well the violence involved in the killing of animals. It was characterized by a doctrine open to all castes and although social hierarchy was accepted it did not emphasize separate social observances but, rather, cut across caste. The idea of conversion was therefore notionally present. The attitude to social hierarchy in most Śramanic sects was not one of radical opposition. In Buddhism, for example, recruitment to the *saṅgha* and support from lay followers was initially in large numbers from the upper castes and the appeal was frequently also made to such groups.[7] Nevertheless there were no restrictions on a lower caste recruitment and in later periods support from such groups was substantial. The founders of the Śramanic sects were not incarnations of deity. Buddhism and Jainism had an ecclesiastical organization, the *saṅgha,* and in most cases there was an overall concern with historicity.

In terms of numbers there appears to have developed even greater support for the Śākta sects which were in many ways antithetical to early Brahmanism. The essentials of Śāktism are sometimes traced back to Harappan times and some of these elements probably went into the making of popular religion from the earliest historical period. Recognized sects gradually crystalized from the first millennium AD when they come to be referred to in the literature of the period. The centrality of worshipping the goddess was initially new to upper caste religion. Some of these

[7] N. Wagle, *Society at the Time of the Buddha* (Bombay, 1966), p. 74.

sects deliberately broke the essential taboos of Brahmanism relating to separate caste functions, commensality, rules of food and drink and sexual taboos.[8] That some of the beliefs of the Śākta sects were later accepted by some *brāhmaṇa* sects is an indication of a break with Vedic religion by these *brāhmaṇa* sects although the legitimacy of the Vedic religion was sometimes sought to be bestowed on the new sects by them. Such religious compromises were not unconnected with the brahmanical need to retain social ascendency. However, some brahmanical sects remained orthodox.

As legitimizers of political authority, the *brāhmaṇas* in the first millennium AD were given grants of land which enabled them to become major landowners. The institutions which emerged out of these grants such as the *agrahāras* became centres of control over rural resources as well as of Brahmanical learning and practice. It was probably this high social and economic status of the *brāhmaṇa* castes which encouraged the modern idea that Brahmanism and Hinduism were synonymous. But that Brahmanism had also to compromise with local cults is evident from the religious articulation of text and temple and from the frequency with which attempts were introduced into Brahmanism to purify the religion in terms of going back to *śruti* and *smṛti*. In the process of acculturation between brahmanic 'high culture' and the 'low culture' of local cults, the perspective is generally limited to that of the Sanskritization of the latter. It might be historically more accurate on occasion to view it as the reverse, as, for example, in the cult of Viṭhṭhala at Pandharpur or that of Jagannātha at Puri.[9]

[8] Curiously, the eating of meat and the drinking of intoxicants was part of the rejection of Brahmanism for these were now abhorent to Brahmanism, a rather different situation from that described in the Vedic texts where *brāhmaṇas* consumed beef and took *soma*.

[9] G.D. Sontheimer, 'Some Memorial Monuments of Western India,' in *German Scholars in India*, II (New Delhi, 1976); S.G. Tulpule, 'The Origin of Viththala: A new Interpretation,' *ABORI*, 1977–78, vols. 58–59, pp. 1009–15; A. Dandekar, 'Pastoralism and the Cult of Viṭhṭhala,' M. Phil. Dissertation,

In such cases the deities of tribals and low caste groups become, for reasons other than the purely religious, centrally significant and Brahmanism has to adapt itself to the concept of such deities. The domain of such deities evolves out of a span spreading horizontally, moving from a village to its networks of exchange and finally encompassing a region. The focal centre of such a cult takes on a political dimension as well in the nature of the control which it exercises, quite apart from ritual and belief. Pilgrimage then becomes a link across various circumferences.

The increasing success of Brahmanism by the end of the first millennium AD resulted in the gradual displacement of Śramanism—but not entirely. Local cults associated with new social groups led to the emergence of the more popular Puranic religion. Vedic deities were subordinated or ousted. Viṣṇu and Śiva came to be worshipped as the pre-eminent deities. The thrust of Puranic religion was in its assimilative and accommodating processes. A multitude of new cults, sects and castes were worked into the social and religious hierarchy. Religious observance often coincided with caste identities.

By the early second millennium AD a variety of devotional cults—referred to by the generic label *bhakti*—had come to form a major new religious expression. They drew on the Puranic tradition of Śaivism and Vaiṣṇavism but were also in varying degrees the inheritors of the Śramanic religions. Their emphasis on complete loyalty to the deity has been seen as a parallel to feudal loyalties. But what was more significant was that *bhakti* cults and the sects which grew around them sought to underline dependence on and release from rebirth through the deity. To this extent they indicate a departure from earlier indigenous religion. These cults were god-centred rather than man-centred. The ritual of sacrifice had been substituted by the worship of an icon. Some sects accepted, up to a point, brahmanical *śruti* and *smṛti* whereas others

JNU; H. Kulke, *Jagannātha kult und Gajapati-Königtum* (Wiesbaden, 1979), p. 227; H. Kulke and D. Rothermund, *A History of India* (London, 1986), p. 145ff.

vehemently denied it, a debate which continues to this day. Those sects in opposition to Brahmanism which sought to transcend caste and differentiated social observances, insisting that every worshipper was equal in the eyes of the deity, often ended up as castes, thus once again coinciding sect with caste. With the arrival of Islam in India some drew from the ideas of Islam. Most of these sects were geographically limited and bound by the barriers of language. Possibly the beginnings of larger religious communities within what is now called the Hindu tradition, date to the middle of the second millennium, such as perhaps some Vaiṣṇava sects, where, for example, the worship of Kṛṣṇa at Mathura drew audiences from a larger geographical region than before. This also heralds a change in the nature of Puranic religion, for Mathura attracts Vaiṣṇavas from eastern and southern India and becomes like Ayodhya (for the worship of Rāma[10]) the focus of a search for sacred topography. It might perhaps be seen as an attempt to go beyond local caste and sect and build a broader community. The historical reasons for its happening at this juncture need to be explored.

Initial opposition from those of high caste status also encouraged *bhakti* sects to inculcate a sense of community within themselves, particularly if they were economically successful, such as the Vīraśaivas. Even when such religious sects attempted to constitute a larger community, the limitations of location, caste and language, acted as a deterrent to a single, homogeneous Hindu community. In the continuing processes of either appropriation or rejection of belief and practice, the kaleidoscopic change in the constitution of religious sects was one which precluded the emergence of a uniform, monolithic religion.

The multiplicity of cults and sects also reflects a multiplicity of beliefs. Even in Brahmanism we are told that if two *śruti* traditions are in conflict then both are to be held as law.[11] This is a

[10] A. Bakker, *Ayodhya* (Groningen, 1984).
[11] Manu II. 14–15.

fundamentally different approach from that of religions which would like to insist on a single interpretation arising out of a given theological framework. This flexibility together with the emphasis on social observance rather than theology allowed of a greater privatization of religion than was possible in most other religions. Renunciatory tendencies were common, were respected and often gave sanction to private forms of worship. The renouncer opted out of society, yet was highly respected.[12] The private domain of belief was always a permissible area of early Indian religion: a religion which is perhaps better seen as primarily the religious belief of social segments, sometimes having to agglomerate and sometimes remaining sharply differentiated. The coexistence of religious sects should not be mistaken for the absorption of all sects into an ultimately unified entity. But the demarcation was often more significant since it related both to differences in religious belief and practice as well as social status and political needs. The status of a sect could change as it was hinged to that of its patrons. Political legitimation through the use of religious groups was recognized, but the appeal was to a particular sect or cult or a range of these and not to a monolithic religion. Royal patronage within the same ruling family, extended to a multiplicity of sects, was probably conditioned as much by the exigencies of political and social requirements as by a religious catholicity. This social dimension as well as the degree to which a religious sect had its identity in caste or alternatively was inclusive of caste, has been largely ignored in the modern interpretation of early Hinduism. With the erosion of social observances and caste identity, there is now a search for a new identity and here the creation of a new Hinduism becomes relevant.

The evolution of Hinduism is not a linear progression from a founder through an organizational system, with sects branching off. It is rather the mosaic of distinct cults, deities, sects and ideas

[12] Romila Thapar, 'Renunciation: The making of a Counter-Culture?,' in *Ancient Indian Social History: Some Interpretations* (Delhi, 1978), pp. 63–104.

and the adjusting, juxtaposing or distancing of these to existing ones, the placement drawing not only on belief and ideas but also on the socio-economic reality. New deities could be created linked genealogically to the established ones, as in the recent case of Santoshi Ma, new rituals worked out and the new sect could become the legitimizer of a new caste. Religious practice and belief are often self-sufficient within the boundaries of a caste and are frequently determined by the needs of a caste. The worship of icons was unthought of in the Vedic religion, but the idol becomes a significant feature of Puranic religion and therefore also in the eyes of contemporary Muslim observers. The consciousness of a similarity in ritual and belief in different geographical regions was not always evident. Thus *bhakti* cults were confined to particular regions and were frequently unaware of their precursors or contemporaries elsewhere. Recourse to historicity of founder and practice was confined within the sect and was not required of a conglomeration of sects which later came to be called Hinduism. This is in part reflected in the use of the term *sampradāya* for a sect where the emphasis is on transmission of traditional belief and usage through a line of teachers. The insistence on proving the historicity of human incarnations of deity, such as Rāma and Kṛṣṇa, is a more recent phenomenon and it may be suggested that there is a subconscious parallel with the prophet and the messiah. The identification of the *janma-bhūmis*, the location of the exact place where Kṛṣṇa and Rāma were born, becomes important only by the mid-second millennium AD.

Religions such as Buddhism, Jainism, Islam and Christianity, see themselves as part of the historical process of the unfolding and interpreting of the single religion and sects are based on variant interpretations of the original teaching. They build their strength on a structure of ecclesiastical organization. In contrast to this, Hindu sects often had a distinct and independent origin. Assimilation was possible and was sometimes expressed in the appropriation of existing civilizational symbols. What needs to be investigated is the degree to which such civilizational symbols were originally religious in connotation.

Civilizational symbols are manifested in many ways: from the symbol of the *svāstika* to the symbol of the renouncer as the noblest and most respected expression of human aspirations. The history of the *svāstika* goes back to the fourth millennium BC where it occurs on seals and impressions from northwest India and Central Asia. In the Indian subcontinent it is not a specifically Hindu symbol for it is used by a variety of religious groups in various ways, but in every case it embodies the auspicious. The Bon-po of the Himalayan borderlands reverse the symbol to distance themselves from the Buddhists. The two epics, the *Mahābhārata* and the *Rāmāyaṇa,* frequently treated as primarily the religious literature of the Vaiṣṇavas, are in origin as epics, civilizational symbols. They were, at one level, the carriers of ethical traditions and were used again by a variety of religious sects to propagate their own particular ethic, a situation which is evident from the diverse treatment of the theme of the *Rāmāyaṇa* in Vālmīki, in the Buddhist *Vessantara* and *Dasaratha Jātakas* and in the Jaina version—the *Paumacaryam* of Vimalasūri.[13] The epic versions were also used for purposes of political legitimation. The primarily Vaiṣṇava religious function of the epics develops gradually and comes to fruition in the second millennium AD with clearly defined sects worshipping Rāma or Kṛṣṇa coinciding with the development of what has been called the Puranic religion. Subsequent to this were various tribal adaptations of the *Rāmāyaṇa,* and these were less concerned with the Vaiṣṇava message and more with articulating their own social fears and aspirations.

Even on the question of beliefs about the after-life, although the concept of *karma* and rebirth was commonly referred to, there were distinct and important groups who believed in a different concept. The life after death of the hero in the heaven of Indra or

[13] Romila Thapar, 'The Rāmāyaṇa: Theme and Variations,' in S.N. Mukherjee, ed., *India: History and Thought* (Calcutta, 1982), pp. 221–53.

Śiva, waited upon by *apsaras*, goes back to the Vedic belief in the *pitṛloka* or House of the Fathers. This belief is a major motivation in the widespread hero cults from the mid-first millennium AD onwards.[14] Here even the concept of after-life was conditioned by social birth and function. A different idea influences the way in which the ritual of *satī* changes its meaning over time. Initially a ritual which ensured that the faithful wife accompanied her hero-husband to heaven, and therefore associated largely with *kṣatriya* castes and those dying heroic deaths, its practice by other castes in the second millennium AD involved a change in eschatology. Ultimately the *satī* was defied, which meant that she neither went to heaven nor was subjected to the rules of *karma*.[15]

It has been suggested that there was a structural similarity in various rituals practised by people in different regions and therefore shared myths and shared ritual patterns can account for some unity in the varieties of the religious beliefs that we find in India over a long time.[16] This is certainly true. But nevertheless it is different from a shared creed, catechism, theology and ecclesiastical organization.

The definition of Hinduism as it has emerged in recent times appears not to have emphasized the variant premises of Indian religion and therefore the difference in essence from the model of Semitic religions. This definition was the result of various factors: of Christian missionaries who saw this as the lacunae of religions in India and which they regarded as primitive; of some Orientalist scholarship anxious to fit the 'Hindu' process into a comprehensible whole based on a known model; the efforts also of Indian reform movements attempting to cleanse Indian religion of what they regarded as negative encrustations and trying to find parallels with the Semitic model. Even in the translation of texts from

[14] Romila Thapar, 'Death and the Hero,' in S.C. Humphreys and H. King, *Mortality and Immortality: The Anthropology and Archaeology of Death* (London, 1981), pp. 293–316.

[15] Romila Thapar, 'Sati in History,' *Seminar*, no. 342 (February 1988).

[16] Personal Communication, B.K. Matilal.

Sanskrit into English, where religious concepts were frequently used the translation often reflected a Christian undertone. The selection of texts to be studied had its own purpose. The East India Company's interest in locating and codifying Hindu law gave a legal form to what was essentially social observance and customary law. The concept of law required that it be defined as a cohesive ideological code. The Manu *Dharmaśāstra,* for example, which was basically part of Brahmanical *smṛti* was taken as the laws of the Hindus and presumed to apply universally. In the process of upward social mobility during the late eighteenth and early nineteenth centuries, traders and artisanal groups emerged as patrons of temple building activities and the trend to conform to the brahmanical model was reinforced by this comprehension of Hinduism.[17] The growth of the political concepts of majority and minority communities further galvanized the process.

The degree to which castes and sects functioned independently even in situations which would elsewhere have been regarded as fundamentally of theological importance, can perhaps be seen in attitudes to religious persecution and the manifestations of intolerance. Among the normative values which were highlighted in the discussion of Hinduism in recent times, has been the concept of *ahimsā* or non-violence. It has been argued that non-violence and tolerance were special features of Hinduism which particularly demarcated its ethics from those of Islam and to a lesser extent Christianity. Yet *ahimsā* as an absolute value is characteristic of certain Śramanic sects and less so of Brahmanism. The notion appears in the *Upaniṣads,* but it was the Buddhists and the Jainas who first made it foundational to their teaching, and their message was very different from that of the *Bhagavad-Gītā* on this matter. That Brahmanism and Śramanism were recognized as distinct after the period of the *Upaniṣads* further underlines the significance of *ahimsā* to Śramanic thinking. This is also borne out by the evidence of religious persecution.

[17] H. Sanyal, *Social Mobility in Bengal* (Calcutta, 1981).

In spite of what historians, ancient and modern, have written, there is a persistent, popular belief that the 'Hindus' never indulged in religious persecution. However, the Śaivite persecution of Śramanic sects is attested to and on occasion, retaliation by the latter. Hsüan Tsang writing in the seventh century refers to this when he describes his visit to Kashmir.[18] That this was not the prejudiced view of the Buddhist pilgrim is made clear by the historian Kalhaṇa in the *Rājataraṅginī*, who even in the twelfth century refers to the earlier destruction of Buddhist monasteries and the killing of Buddhist monks by the Hūna king Mihīrakula and other ardent Śaivites.[19] That Mihīrakula was a Hūna is used by modern historians to excuse these actions, but it should be remembered that he gave large grants of land, *agrahāras*, to the *brāhmaṇas* of Gandhāra, which Kalhaṇa in disgust informs us they gratefully received. Clearly there was competition for royal patronage and the Śaiva *brāhmaṇas* triumphed over the Buddhists. The Buddhist association with the commerce between India and Central Asia was one of the reasons for the material prosperity of the Buddhist *saṅgha*.[20] The Hūna disruption of the Indian trade with Central Asia may well have resulted in an antagonism between the northern Buddhists and the Hūnas.

Elsewhere there is a variation on this story. In Tamil Nadu, for example, from the seventh century onwards, Śaiva sects attacked Jaina establishments and eventually succeeded in driving out the *śramaṇas*.[21] In neighbouring Karnataka, at a somewhat later date, the Vīraśaivas or Lingāyatas acquiring wealth and status in commerce, persecuted Jaina monks and destroyed Jaina images.[22] In

[18] S. Beal, *Si-yu-ki*, I. xcix.

[19] I. 307.

[20] Xinru Liu, *Ancient India and Ancient China* (Delhi, 1988).

[21] Romila Thapar, *Cultural Transaction and Early India* (Delhi, 1987), p. 17ff.

[22] P.B. Desai, *Jainism in South India* (Sholapur, 1957), pp. 23, 63, 82–3, 124, 397–402; *Epigraphia Indica* V, p. 142ff, 255; *Ep. Ind.* XXIX, pp. 139–44; *Annual Report of South Indian Epigraphy*, 1923, p. 4ff.

some inscriptions the Vīraśaivas claim that the Jainas began the trouble. In this case the hostility can be traced not to competition for royal patronage but rather to control of the commercial economy over which the Jainas had a substantial hold. A further reason may also have been linked to the fact that the Jainas, maintaining high standards of literacy, may have been seen by the Vīraśaivas as rivals in the role of advisers and administrators at the royal court.

What is significant about this persecution is that it involved not all the Śaivas but particular segments of sects among them. The persecution was not a *jehād* or a holy war or a crusade in which all Hindu sects saw it as their duty to support the attack or to wage war against the Buddhists or the Jainas. Nor was there room for an inquisition in the Indian situation, for there dissidents could found a new sect and take on a splinter caste status. The notion of heresy evolved gradually. The term *pasamda* in the Aśokan edicts refers merely to any religious sect or philosophical school. By the time of the Puranic literature, *pāṣaṇḍa* quite clearly referred to sects in opposition to Brahmanism and carried with it the clear connotation of contempt.[23] Untouchability was also a form of religious persecution, for this exclusion was common to Brahmanism as well as to some Śramanic sects, the *caṇḍāla* being a category apart. Vaiṣṇavism, although it had its episodes of enemity with Śaivism and others, seems to have been less prone to persecuting competitors. Instead it resorted to assimilating other cults and used the notion of the *avatāra* or incarnation of Viṣṇu to great effect in doing so. But even Vaiṣṇavism was less given to assimilating the Śramanic sects, preferring to absorb tribal and folk cults and epic heroes. Thus in spite of the reference to Buddha as among the ten incarnations, this, interestingly, does not become the focus of a large body of myths or Puranic texts as do the other incarnations. If acts of intolerance and violence against other religious sects reflecting the consciousness of belonging to a religious community

[23] Romila Thapar, 'Renunciation'.

did not form part of a Hindu stand against such sects, then it also raises the question of how viable is the notion of a Hindu community for this early period.

The notion of a Hindu community does not have as long an ancestry as is often presumed. Even in the normative texts of Brahmanism, the *Dharmaśāstras*, it is conceded that there were a variety of communities, determined by location, occupation and caste, none of which were necessarily bound together by a common religious identity. The term for village, *grāma*, referred to the collective inhabitants of a place and included cultivators and craftsmen. The control of this community lay in the hands of the *grāma-saṅgha*[24] and the *mahājana* and, in some cases, the *pañcakula*. Customary law of the village is referred to as *grāma-dharma*.[25] The sense of the village as the community was further impressed by the grants of land to *brāhmaṇas* and officers in the late first millennium AD when they began to be given administrative and judicial rights over the villages granted to them. Community therefore had one of its roots in location and the law of the *janapada* / territory is listed among those which a king should observe.

In urban centres, craftsmen of the same profession or of related professions formed organizations and guilds, such as the *pūga*, *goṣṭhi* and *śreṇī*. They were responsible for production and sale and gradually took on a community character. Thus donations were made at Buddhist *stūpas*, as the one at Sanchi, by *goṣṭhis* and *śreṇīs* which identified themselves as such.[26] These communities were part of the larger Buddhist community and the same *stūpa*

[24] Manu VIII. 41.

[25] *Aśvalāyana Gṛhasūtra* I.7.I.; *Aśvalāyana Śrauta-sūtra* XII.8; Pāṇiṇi 6.2.62; *Amarakośa* 2.3.19; Buddhist texts speak more specifically of village boundaries (*Vinaya Piṭaka* I. 109. 10; III. 46.200). This was necessary in a system where the limits of areas for collecting alms had to be defined for each monastery.

[26] See inscriptions from Sanchi as given in J. Marshall and A. Foucher, *Monuments of Sanchi* (Calcutta, 1940); also H. Lüders, *Ep. Ind.* X. nos. 162–907; See also the Bhattiprolu inscription, Luders no. 1332.

was embellished from donations by a number of other such communities and by individuals. One can therefore speak of a Buddhist community which cuts across the boundaries of caste and locality. In contrast is the silk-weavers guild at Mandasor which built a temple to Sūrya, the Sun-god, and rennovated it in the late fifth century AD.[27] Even though the members of this guild had taken to a variety of alternative professions they retained their identity as a guild for the purpose of building a temple. This religious edifice was built through the effort of a single group, identified as a guild and worshipping Sūrya, for no other Sun-worshippers were involved nor any other religious group which today would be called Hindu. It is unlikely that such a group saw itself as part of a larger Hindu community as its identity seems to have been deliberately limited. The Hūnas established themselves in the region soon after and were known to be Sun-worshippers. A temple to the Sun was built at Gwalior in the early sixth century AD by a high-ranking individual.[28] Curiously there is neither contribution from nor reference to other Sun-worshipping communities in the area in the later inscription, barring the reference to the Hūna kings.

In urban life the guild was a commanding institution acting as the nucleus of the urban community. The coins and seals of such guilds point to economic power and social status.[29] The *Nārada-smṛti* clearly states that a guild could frame its own laws and these laws related both to administration and social usage.[30] The customary law of the guild, the *śrenī-dharma*, is particularly mentioned in the *Dharmaśāstras* and to which kings are required to conform. The importance of the guild also lies in the fact that some evolved into *jātis* or castes, becoming units of endogamous mar-

[27] J.F. Fleet, ed., *Inscriptions of the Early Gupta Kings and their Successors*, Corpus Inscriptionum Indicarum, III (Varanasi, 1970 reprint), p. 79ff.

[28] *Ibid.*, p. 162ff.

[29] *Bṛhaspati* I. 28–30; *Kātyayaṇa* 2.82; 17.18; I. 126; Archaeological Survey of India, Annual Report, 1903–04; 1911–12.

[30] *Nārada-smṛti*, X. 1–2; *Ep. Ind.* XXX, p. 169.

riage uniting kinship and profession. Those not following a Śramanic religion maintained their own separate religious identity. We are also told that the king must respect *jāti-dharma*. The emphasis on the *dharma* of the *janapada* (locality or territory) *śreṇī* (guild) and *jāti* (caste) and the absence of reference to the *dharma* of various religious sects or of a conglomeration of religious sects are a pointer perhaps to what actually constituted the sense of community in the early past.

Identities were, in contrast to the modern nation state, segmented identities. The notion of community was not absent but there were multiple communities identified by locality, languages, caste, occupation and sect. What appears to have been absent was the notion of a uniform, religious community readily identified as Hindu. The first occurrence of the term 'Hindu' is as a geographical nomenclature and this has its own significance. This is not a quibble since it involves the question of the historical concept of 'Hindu'. Inscriptions of the Achaemenid empire refer to the frontier region of the Indus or Sindhu as Hi(n)dush.[31] Its more common occurrence many centuries later is in Arabic texts where the term is initially used neither for a religion nor for a culture. It refers to the inhabitants of the Indian subcontinet, the land across the Sindhu or Indus river. Al-Hind was therefore a geographical identity and the Hindus were all the people who lived on this land. Hindu thus essentially came to mean 'the other' in the eyes of the new arrivals. It was only gradually and over time that it was used not only for those who were inhabitants of India but also for those who professed a religion other than Islam or Christianity. In this sense Hindu included both the *brāhmaṇa*s and the lower castes, an inclusion which was contrary to the precepts of Brahmanism. This all-inclusive term was doubtless a new and bewildering feature for the multiple sects and castes who generally saw themselves as separate entities.

The people of India curiously do not seem to have perceived

[31] The Persepolis and Naqsh-i-Rustam inscriptions of Darius, in D.C. Sircar, *Select Inscriptions*, vol. I (Calcutta, 1965), p. 7.

the new arrivals as a unified body of Muslims. The name 'Muslim' does not occur in the records of early contacts. The term used was either ethnic, Turuṣka, referring to the Turks,[32] or geographical, Yavana,[33] or cultural, *mleccha*. Yavana, a back formation from *yona* had been used since the first millennium BC for Greeks and others coming from West Asia. *Mleccha* meaning impure, goes back to the Vedic texts and referred to non-Sanskrit speaking people often outside the caste hierarchy or regarded as foreign and was extended to include low castes and tribals. Foreigners, even of high rank, were regarded as *mleccha*.[34] A late fifteenth-century inscription from Mewar refers to the Sultan of Malwa and his armies as *Śakas*, a term used many centuries before for the Scythians, and therefore reflecting a curious undertow of historical memory.[35] These varying terms, each seeped in historical meaning, do not suggest a monolithic view, but rather a diversity of perceptions which need to be enquired into more fully.

For the early Muslim migrants Indian society was also a puzzle, for it was the first where large numbers did not convert to Islam. There was, further, the unique situation that they were faced with a society which had no place for the concept of conversion, for one's birth into a caste defines one's religious identity and conversion is outside the explanation of belief.

Historians have posited two monolithic religions, Hinduism

[32] Similarly Muslim women were often referred to as *turuṣki*, as, for example, in Hemādri, *Caturvarga-cintāmaṇi*, Prāyaścitta-kāṇḍa.

[33] e.g. Chateśvara temple inscriptions, where in the thirteenth century a reference is made to a campaign against the *yavanas*. *Ep. Ind.* 1952, XXIX, pp. 121–2.

[34] Romila Thapar, 'The Image of the Barbarian in Early India,' in *Ancient Indian Social History*, pp. 152–92. A fourteenth-century inscription from Delhi refers to Shahab-ud-din, as a *mleccha*, who was the first Turuṣka to rule Dhillika/Delhi. D.R. Bhandarkar, ed., Appendix to *Epi. Ind.* XIX–XXIII, no. 683.

[35] Udaipur inscription of the time of Rajamalla in *Bhavnagar Inscriptions*, p. 117ff. And see Bhandarkar, ed., Appendix to *Ep. Ind.* XIX–XXIII, no. 862. It is ironic that it was earlier thought that these Rajput ruling families may in some cases have had their origin in the Śakas!

and Islam, coming face to face in the second millennium AD. This projection requires re-examination since it appears to be based on a somewhat simplistic reading of the court chronicles of the Sultans. These spoke of Hindus sometimes in the sense of the indigenous population, sometimes as a geographical entity and sometimes as followers of a non-Islamic religion. Such references should be read in their specific meaning and not as referring uniformly to the religion of India. Possibly the germ of the idea of a Hindu community begins when people start referring to themselves as Hindus, perhaps initially as a concession to being regarded as 'the other'. Such usage in non-Islamic sources is known from the fifteenth century. The literature of the *bhakti* sects registers a variation on this. Much that was composed in an indigenous tradition such as the *Rāmacaritamānas* of Tulsidās seems not to use the term Hindu. That which was clearly influenced by Islamic ideas such as the verses of Kabīr refers to Hindus and counterposes Hindus and Turuṣkas in a religious sense. Curiously both Tulsidās and Kabīr belonged to the Rāmanandin sect, yet expressed themselves in very different idioms.

Rānā Kumbha of Mewar ruling in the fifteenth century, on defeating the sultans of Dhilli and Gurjarātra, takes the title of *himdu suratrāna*,[36] *suratrāna*, being the Sanskrit for sultan. In the context of the inscription in which it occurs, it is less a declaration of religious identity and more a claim to being a sultan of *al-hind*, superior to the other sultans. In another inscription the sultan of Gujarat is referred to as the *gurjareśvara* and the *gurjarādhīṣvara*, but the virtually hereditary enemy, the sultan of Malwa, merely as *suratrāna*,[37] a subtle but significant distinction.

It would also be worthwhile to investigate when the term Muslim came to be used in what would now be called Hindu sources. One's suspicion is that Turuṣka and its variants and

[36] Sadadi Jaina inscription of the time of Kumbhakarṇa of Medapata in *Bhavnagar Inscriptions*, p. 114ff and D.R. Bhandarkar, *op. cit.*, no. 784; D. Sharma, *Lectures on Rajput History and Culture* (Delhi, 1970), p. 55.

[37] Kīrtistambha-praśasti, *ASIR*, XXIII, p. 111ff.

certainly *mleccha* were more commonly used as they are to this day. *Mleccha* does not have a primary religious connotation. It is a signal of social and cultural difference. Indian Muslims of course did not discontinue caste affiliations, particularly as the basis of marriage relations and often even occupations. Thus the gulf between the high caste Muslims claiming foreign descent, such as the *ashrafs*, and the rest was not altogether dissimilar to the social difference between *brāhmaṇa*s and non-*brāhmaṇa*s. But the rank and file were often converted from lower castes, where an entire *jāti* would convert. These Muslims retained their local language in preference to Persian, were recognized by minor differences of dress and manner and often incorporated their earlier rituals and mythology into Islamic tradition. Some of the *mangal-kābyas* in Bengali, for instance, are an example of such interlinks in the creation of what might be seen as a new mythology where Puranic deities intermingled with the personalities of the Quran.[38] This becomes even more evident in the folk literature of regions with a large Muslim population. Elsewhere in Tamil-Nadu, for instance, the guardian figures in the cult of Draupadi are Muslim.[39] This is not an anomaly if it is seen in terms of local caste relations.

This is not to suggest that the relationship was one of peaceful coexistence or total cultural integration but rather that the perception which groups subscribing to Hindu and Islamic symbols had of each other was not in terms of a monolithic religion, but more in terms of distinct and disparate castes and sects along a social continuum. Even the recognition of a religious identity does not automatically establish a religious community. Tensions, confrontations and even persecutions at the level of political authority were not necessarily repeated all the way down the social scale nor were all caste and sectarian conflicts reflected at the upper levels. Clashes which on the face of it would now be interpreted as between Hindus and Muslims, would require a deeper investiga-

[38] Ashim Roy, *The Islamic Syncretistic Tradition in Bengal* (Princeton, 1983).
[39] A. Hiltebeitel, *The Cult of Draupadi* (Chicago, 1988).

tion to ascertain how far they were clashes between specific castes and sects and to what degree did they involve support and sympathy from other castes and sects identifying with the same religion or seeking such identity.

The nineteenth-century definition of the Hindu community sought its justification in early history using Mill's periodization which assumes the existence of Hindu and Muslim communities and takes the history of the former back to the centuries BC. Its roots were provided by yet another nineteenth-century obsession, that of the theory of Aryan race.[40] It was argued that the Indo-Aryans conquered India and created the Hindu religion and civilization. In the theory of Aryan race the nineteenth-century concern with European origins was transferred to India. The theory as applied to India emphasized the arrival of a superior, conquering race of Aryans who used the mechanism of caste to segregate groups racially.[41] It underlined upper caste superiority by arguing that they were the descendants of the Aryans and it therefore became an acceptable explanation of the origin of upper castes, who could now also claim relationship to the European Aryans.[42] The lower castes were seen as the non-Aryan, indigenous people and were said to be of Dravidian and Austric origin. Aryanism was seen then to define the true and pure Hindu community. Other groups recruited into the caste structure at lower levels were regarded as polluting the pristine Hindu community.

Because of its centrality to both the notion of community and religion, the theory of Aryan race requires to be looked at critically by historians working on nineteenth-century ideas as well as historians of ancient India. The earlier evidence quoted in support of the theory as applied to India begins to fade with information

[40] Romila Thapar, 'Ideology and the Interpretation of Early Indian History,' of this volume, p. 1ff.

[41] H. Risley, *The People of India* (London, 1908).

[42] As, for example, in the writings of Keshab Chunder Sen, 'Philosophy and Madness in Religion,' in *Keshab Chunder Sen's Lectures in India* (London, 1901).

from archaeology and linguistics. The notion of an Aryan race has now been generally discarded in scholarship and what we are left with is essentially a linguistic category: the Indo-Aryan speaking people. The archaeological picture takes the foundation of Indian civilization back to proto-history and the Harappa culture. The characteristic features of the latter do not mesh with those of the Vedic texts associated with the culture of the Indo-Aryan speakers.[43] The culture depicted in the Vedic texts seems increasingly to have drawn on local practices and beliefs, some going back to the Harappa culture or earlier, others drawing perhaps from the then contemporary society in India. There is virtually no evidence of the invasion and conquest of northwestern India by a dominant culture coming from across the border. Most sites register a gradual change of archaeological cultures. Where there is evidence of destruction and burning it could as easily have been a local activity and is not indicative of a large-scale invasion. The border lands of the northwest were in communication with Iran and Central Asia even before the Harappa culture with evidence of the passage of goods and ideas across the region.[44] This situation continued into later times and if seen in this light then the intermittent arrival of groups of Indo-European speakers in the northwest, perhaps as pastoralists or farmers or itinerant traders, would pose little problem. It is equally plausible that in some cases local languages became Indo-Europeanized through contact. Such situations would require a different kind of investigation. If cultural elements from elsewhere are being assessed, then during the Harappan period excavated evidence for contact with West Asia via the Gulf was more significant than that with eastern Iran and Central Asia and this raises another set of possibilities.

[43] Romila Thapar, 'The Study of Society in India,' in *Ancient Indian Social History*, pp. 211–39; also, 'The Archaeological Background to the Agnicayana Ritual,' in F. Staal, *Agni*, vol. II (Berkeley, 1983), pp. 3–40.

[44] J. Jarrige, 'Excavations at Mehrgarh: their Significance for Understanding the Background of the Harappan Civilisation,' in G. Possehl, ed., *Harappan Civilisation* (New Delhi, 1982), p. 79ff.

The more basic question for the historian is to explain the slow and gradual spread of the Indo-Aryan language across a large part of the Indian subcontinet. Here again the evidence from linguistics provides an interesting pointer. The claim that the earliest of the Vedic texts, the *Ṛg Veda* dating back to the second millennium BC is linguistically purely Indo-Aryan is now under question for it is being argued that the text already registers the presence of non-Aryan speakers. The later Vedic texts show an even greater admixture of non-Aryan and specifically when dealing with certain areas of activity, such as agriculture.[45] The emergent picture might suggest that the speakers of Indo-Aryan may have been in a symbiotic relationship with speakers of non-Aryan languages, with a mutual adopting of not only vocabulary and linguistic structures in a bi-lingual situation but also technologies and religious practices and beliefs.[46] The exclusivity of *brāhmaṇa* ritual does not have to be explained on the basis of a racial segregation, but can be viewed as derived from the will to retain a certain kind of priestly power, which, claiming bestowal by the deities would ensure a separate and special status. Possibly the political hold of priestly power has its roots in the Harappa culture. In charting the spread of Indo-Aryan it is worth remembering that Sanskrit not only underwent change in relation to other languages with which it had to co-exist and in relation to social change but that its use was initially restricted to *brāhmaṇa* ritual and elite groups.

The focus therefore is shifting to an investigation of the many ways in which a language gains acceptability. This would involve detailed studies of the juxtaposition of new technologies particularly in relation to ecological contexts, of demography, of kinship systems and the ways in which social groups interact where stratification relates to lineage rather than to race. So deep has been the modern obsession with race that Pargiter as late as in the 1920s suggested the identification of even the traditional de-

[45] T. Burrow, *The Sanskrit Language* (London, 1965), p. 379: M.M. Deshpande and P.E. Hook, eds., *Aryan and non-Aryan in India* (Michigan, 1979).

[46] Romila Thapar, *From Lineage to State* (New Delhi, 1984), p. 21ff.

scent groups from the genealogies of the Puranic texts as Aryan, Dravidian and Austric.[47] Thus the spread of the Indo-Aryan languages and the changes they manifest are a far more complicated study than that implied in the theory of spread by conquest. There is also a need to see the evolving of early Indian society as suggested by archaeological evidence independent of the attempt to impose Aryan identities on archaeological cultures. Only then can we hope to understand the social processes which went into the creation of early Indian society. In the text the term *ārya* generally refers to status indicating one who is to be respected. Whereas the connotation of *dāsa* may be said to contain racial elements, as for example, in the emphasis on physical characteristics, such elements are not in the forefront of references to *ārya*. Thus in the Vedic texts there are *ārya*s of *dāsa* descent, the *dāsi-putrāḥ brāhmaṇas*,[48] or, politically powerful *dāsa* chiefs making gifts to the *brāhmaṇas*.[49] (It is interesting that one of the most respected lineages, that of the Pūrus is associated with sub-standard Sanskrit.[50] It is also said that Pūru was an ancient king who was an Asura Rākṣasa and was overthrown by Bharata,[51] which can hardly be said to place the Pūrus in the category of the pure Aryans! In the *Dharmaśāstras* it is the observance of the complex *varnāśrama-dharma* which defines the *ārya*. To trace the emergence of caste would also involve a study of access to resources, kinship and clan networks and notions of pollution.

Early history suggests the existence of multiple communities based on various identities. The need to create the idea of a single, Hindu community appears to have been a concern of more recent times which was sought to be justified by recourse to a particular

[47] F.E. Pargiter, *Ancient Indian Historical Tradition* (London, 1922).

[48] *Bṛhaddevatā* 4.11–15; 21–3; describes the birth of Dīrghatamas and his son Kakśivant as the son of a *dāsi*. The *Aitareya Brāhmaṇa* 2.19 and the *Kauśītaki Brāhmaṇa* 12.3 describe the Ṛg Vedic seer Kavasa Ailusa as a *dāsi-putraḥ*.

[49] Romila Thapar, *From Lineage to State*, p. 43.

[50] *Ṛg Veda*. VII. 18.13.

[51] *Śatapatha Brāhmaṇa* VI. 8.I.14.

construction of history. The new Hinduism which is now sought to be projected as the religion of this community is in many ways a departure from the earlier religious sects. It seeks historicity for the incarnations of its deities, encourages the idea of a centrally sacred book, claims monotheism as significant to the worship of deity, acknowledges the authority of the ecclesiastical organization of certain sects as prevailing over all and has supported large-scale missionary work and conversion. These changes allow it to transcend caste identities and reach out to larger numbers. Religions indigenous to India which questioned brahmanical belief and practice such as Buddhism and Jainism have been inducted into Hinduism and their separateness is either denied or ignored. Pre-Islamic India is therefore presented as a civilization characterized by an inclusive Hinduism, whereas it would seem that the reality perhaps lay in looking at it as a cluster of distinctive sects and cults, observing common civilizational symbols but with belief and ritual ranging from atheism to animism and a variety of religious organizations identifying themselves by location, language and caste. Even the sense of religious identity seems to have related more closely to sect than to a dominant Hindu community.

The modern construction of Hinduism is often acclaimed as in the following defence of Orientalism: 'The work of integrating a vast collection of myths, beliefs, rituals and laws into a coherent religion and of shaping an amorphous heritage into a rational faith known now as "Hinduism" were endeavours initiated by Orientalists.'[52] Given that religious traditions are constantly reformulated, the particular construction of Hinduism in the last two centuries has an obvious historical causation. Deriving largely from the Orientalist construction of Hinduism, emergent national consciousness appropriated this definition of Hinduism as well as what it regarded as the heritage of Hindu culture. Hindu identity was defined by those who were part of this national consciousness

[52] D. Knopf, 'Hermeneutics versus History,' *Journal of Asian Studies*, 1980, 39.3, pp. 495–505.

and drew on their own idealized image of themselves resulting in an upper-caste, *brāhmaṇa*-dominated identity. Even the counterposing of Hindu to other religious identities as an essential fact of social and historical reality grew out of this construction. But this construction not only deviates from the history of the religious groups involved but fails to encapsulate the essential differences within what is called the Hindu tradition whose presuppositions were distinct from other religions and closely entwined with social articulation. The search for coherence and rational faith was in terms of a perspective familiar to those who came from a Christian religious tradition and hardly reflected any attempt to understand the coherence of a different, indigenous religious tradition. The shape thus given to the latter has changed what originally existed and has made it difficult to recognize the actual earlier form.

The need for postulating a Hindu community became a requirement for political mobilization in the nineteenth century when representation by religious community became a key to power and where such representation gave access to economic resources. The competition for middle class employment brought with it the argument that in all fairness the size of the community should be taken into consideration. Communal representation of the religious kind firmed up the image. Once this argument was conceded it became necessary to recruit as many people as possible into the community. Here the vagueness of what constitutes a Hindu was to the advantage of those propagating a Hindu community. It encouraged an almost new perception of the social and political uses of religion. Conversion to Hinduism was invented largely to bring in the untouchables and the tribals. The notion of purification, *śuddhi*, permitted those who had been converted to Islam and Christianity to be reintroduced to the Hindu fold. A Hindu community with a common identity would be politically powerful. Since it was easy to recognize other communities on the basis of religion, such as Muslims and Christians, an effort was made to consolidate a parallel Hindu community. This involved a change from the earlier segmented identities to one which encompassed caste and region and identified itself by religion which had to be refashioned so as to provide the ideology which would bind the group. In Gramsci's terms, the class which wishes to become hegemonic has to nationalize itself and the new 'nationalist' Hinduism comes from the middle class.

The change implicit in the various levels of what is called modernization inevitably results in the refashioning of communities. Given that the notion of expansive communities may well be imagined, nevertheless the premises on which such communities are constructed are open to analysis and where they claim an historical basis, there the historian has perforce to be involved. This involvement becomes even more necessary when the concept of communities is brought into play in assigning positions to them in history either close to or distant from what are regarded as national aspirations. Thus the majority community tends to define national aspirations. The minority communities in varying degrees are viewed as disrupting society by their refusal to conform. The projection of such communities historically is that of their always having been alien to the dominant culture and therefore refusing to assimilate with the majority.

Minority communities pick up their cue in a similar reconstruction of history seeking to project a unified community stance in all historical situations. The fear of being overwhelmed by the majority community is expressed even in opposition to the making of homogeneous civil laws. These are treated as threats to a specific culture and practice, and there is a tendency to preserve even that which is archaic in an effort to assert a separate identity.

If the history of religions in India is seen as the articulation not only of ideas and rituals but also the perceptions and motivations of social groups, the perspectives which would follow might be different from those with which we are familiar. The discourse and the play between and among religious sects of various kinds, has been a central fact of Indian religion and would reflect a more realistic portrayal of the role of religion in society. A historically analytical enquiry into the definition and role of religion and the concept of religious communities in pre-modern India could be juxtaposed with the way in which these have been perceived by interpreters of the past in the last couple of centuries. Incidentally such an assessment would be valuable not only to contemporary society in India but also to those societies which now host the vast Indian diaspora. Communal ideologies may be rooted in the homeland but also find sustenance in the diaspora.

It is possible now to look more analytically at the perspectives on early Indian society as available in the sources, keeping in mind the insights which we have, arising from research which, in a sense, is being gradually liberated from the polemics of the colonial age. Where institutions and ideologies of modern times seek legitimacy from the early past, at least there, the dialogue between historians working on these time periods becomes imperative.

The Contribution of D.D. Kosambi to Indology

It has recently been argued that a revolution in scientific knowledge comes about not through the accumulation of data alone but through a change in the paradigm.[1] When the framework of explanation or the hypothesis is altered or a new set of questions are posed only then can there be a breakthrough in scientific knowledge. This applies as much to history and the social sciences. The accumulation of data is of course a necessary first step and includes the deriving of fresh data from new sources, but an advance in knowledge is dependent on using the data to present new formulations.

Histories of the Indian sub-continent, such as were to become germane to the perception on the Indian past, have subscribed to three major changes of paradigm. The first comprehensive history was James Mill's *History of British India*[2] published in the early nineteenth century, where he set out his theory of Indian history evolving out of three civilizations, the Hindu, the Muslim and the British. The first two of these he described as backward, stagnant and ahistoric. His theory was to become axiomatic to the periodization of Indian history and is with us still, though sometimes in a disguised form. A change came about with Vincent Smith's

[1] T. Kuhn, *The Structure of Scientific Revolutions* (Chicago, 1970).
[2] J. Mill, *History of British India* (London, 1918–23).

History of India[3] published in 1919, which tried to avoid the sharpness of Mill's value judgements. Smith concentrated more on a chronological overview which was in any case less charged with colonial and anti-colonial sentiment and argued for the rise and fall of dynasties as being crucial to the study of Indian history. By the early twentieth century chronological data had accumulated to the point where such a treatment of history was possible. Where Mill's assessment was seeking to justify the British conquest of India, Smith was justifying colonial rule. The infrequency of explicitly negative value judgements on the pre-British period was largely an indication of his awareness of Indian national sentiment in the matter. Nationalist historians writing on early India reversed the value judgements but adhered to the paradigm of dynastic and chronological concerns.

Kosambi's first book, *An Introduction to the Study of Indian History*[4] published in 1956, was a major shift in the paradigm. He had little use for a chronological narrative since he argued that chronology for the early period was too obscure to be meaningful. For him history was the presentation in chronological order of successive developments in the means and relations of production.[5] Because of the absence of reliable historical records he argued that Indian history would have to use the comparative method.[6] This meant a familiarity with a wide range of historical work and his own familiarity with classical European history is evident in his writing; it also meant the use of various disciplines and interdisciplinary techniques to enable the historian to understand the pattern of social formations. His definition of the comparative method required the historian to be an inter-disciplinary creature in himself with the ability to use a large number of

[3] V. Smith, *The Oxford History of India* (Oxford, 1919).

[4] D.D. Kosambi, *An Introduction to the Study of Indian History* (Bombay, 1956). Henceforth *ISIH*.

[5] *Ibid.*, p. 1ff.

[6] *Ibid.*, p. 5ff; 'Combined Methods in Indology' *Indo-Iranian Journal*, 1963, VI, pp. 177–202.

investigative techniques. This ability he demonstrated to the full in his writings on Indology. Added to this was his conviction that the historian in India was in a particularly happy position since so much of the past survives in the present. As he puts it,' . . . the country has one tremendous advantage that was not utilised till recently by the historians: the survival within different social layers of many forms that allow the reconstruction of totally diverse earlier stages.'[7] For him this amply made up for the absence of reliable historical records.

Kosambi's acknowledged status as an Indologist was all the more remarkable, in that by profession he was a mathematician. Indology to begin with was a subsidiary interest, perhaps inherited from his father, a scholar of Pāli and Buddhism who taught at various centres in India, apart from a period at Harvard. The older Kosambi walked the countryside in an effort to relate the texts to their original milieu, an approach which was followed by his son. A quick perusal of the younger Kosambi's many publications, points to a telling trend. His earliest papers in the 1930's sare mainly on various aspects of mathematics. In the 1940's his interest in Indology become apparent in the form of occasional papers. (This was also the period when he wrote on Soviet contributions to mathematics and genetics and was enthusiastic about the Soviet attempt to build a socialist society). He was appointed to the Mathematics' Chair at the T.I.F.R. in 1946. During the 1950's however and until his death in 1966, most of his publications were on Indology and early Indian history although his mathematical interests remained constant.

Given the fact that Indology is now viewed as rooted in a colonial perception of the past, and since Kosambi's writing challenged this perspective, it would be more appropriate to refer to him as a historian, the field in which his major contribution lay and where he has been strikingly influential. But he was prolific and researched into other related areas as well, hence the continuing use of the label, Indologist. His first venture into early Indian sources was a critical assessment of Bhartṛhari which can be regarded as a model

[7] D.D. Kosambi, *The Culture and Civilisation of Ancient India in Historical Outline* (london, 1965). Henceforth *CCAIHO*.

for such analysis.[8] At a later stage he edited, jointly with V.V. Gokhale, the Vidyākara *Subhāśita-ratna-koṣa* for the Harvard Oriental Series.[9] Apart from applying the norms of higher criticism to such texts he also tried to place them in historical context not merely through a chronological analysis but by referring them to the society from which they emanated. He argued that from the first millennium AD Sanskrit should be seen as a measure and expression of upper class unity when it replaced Prākrit in the royal courts and was patronized, particularly in the initial stages, by foreign rulers. This is of course evident in the change from Prākrit to Sanskrit as the language of royal inscriptions between the Mauryan and the Gupta periods. He stressed the feudal background of many Sanskrit texts which brought him into a lively controversy with one of his closest friends, the Harvard Sanskritist, Daniel Ingalls. Kosambi maintained that Sanskrit was deliberately kept restricted to a small number of people, even though the excellent early grammar of the language by Pāṇini, commented upon by Patañjali, converted it into an orderly and systematic language, open to anyone who was taught it properly. However he felt that it froze in the hands of what he called, 'a disdainful priest class',[10] and much of the real world was byepassed in the courtly literature.

The relation of text to context was examined at greater length in his papers on the *Bhagavad Gītā* where he attempted to relate ideology to society.[11] He argued that the *Gītā* in propounding the concept of

[8] 'Some Extant Versions of Bhartrhari's *Śatakas*' *JBBRAS*, 1945, XXI, pp. 17–32; *The Śatakatrayam of Bhartrhari with the commentary of Rāmarṣi*, ed., in collaboration with Pt. K.V. Krishnamoorthi Sharma, Anandāsrama Sanskrit Series No. 127 (Poona, 1947); *The Southern Archetype of Epigrams ascribed to Bhartṛhari*, Bharatiya Vidya Series, 9 (Bombay, 1946); 'The Quality of Renunciation in Bhartṛhari's Poetry,' in *Exasperating Essays* (Poona, 1857), p. 72ff.

[9] Harvard Oriental Series No. 44 (Cambridge Mass., 1956).

[10] *ISIH*, p. 266.

[11] 'The Avatāra Syncretism and possible sources of the Bhagavad Gītā' *JBBRAS*, 1948–9, XXIV-XXV, pp. 121–34; 'Social and Economic Aspects of the Bhagavad Gītā' in *Myth and Reality* (Bombay, 1962), p. 12ff.

bhakti laid emphasis on unquestioning faith in, and personal loyalty and devotion to, a deity, and these values were in conformity with the ideology of feudalism which also required a chain of unquestioning loyalties. The text emphasized caste functions and the requirement to do one's ordained duty as a member of a particular caste which he saw as a message in support of caste society and the conservatism which such a society entails; a message propounded by the upper castes to keep the rest of society passive. He further suggests that religious sects supporting a synthesis of gods and of tolerance are expressions of a period of a social surplus, when wealth was more widely distributed; whereas the ideology of *bhakti* is more frequent in periods of crisis, but that it nevertheless acted as a means of inter-relating the scattered religious beliefs of a region. It could be argued however that the *bhakti* endorsed by the *Gītā* is not identical with that which was taught by later *bhakti* teachers. Whereas the single minded devotion to a deity is retained, the social context changes substantially and is expressed in a concern with a universal ethic which echoes that of the Buddhist and Jainas and which permits the *bhakti* movements to become powerful mobilizers of various social groups. There is an almost apparent contradiction between the emphasis on caste-duty in the *Gītā* and the universal ethic of the later *bhakti* movement.

In his handling of Buddhist texts Kosambi uses them mainly to draw out data on social and economic life and much of his discussion on early trade, for instance, is based on these sources. This was not new as such data had earlier been extracted from these sources by scholars of Buddhism such as Rhys Davids[12] and Fick.[13] Kosambi co-related this data with evidence from Sanskrit sources but above all from archaeological excavations and contemporary inscriptions and brought the Buddhist material into the wider orbit of reconstructing the history of the late first millennium BC. The fact that the Buddhist sources do at times contradict

[12] *Buddhist India* (London, 1903).

[13] *The Social Organisation in North East India in Buddha's Time* (Calcutta, 1920).

the brahmanical tradition was for him a particularly important aspect of the Pāli texts and invested them with the kind of authenticity which he found invaluable. The recognition of this feature he owed to his father's work on the Buddhist texts.[14]

His knowledge of Sanskrit led Kosambi to a series of etymological analyses which he used to great effect in reconstructing the social background, particularly of the Vedic period.[15] Thus he argued that the names of many of the established *brāhmaṇas* in Vedic literature and the Purāṇic tradition clearly pointed to their being of non-Aryan origin. Some were given the epithet, *dāsi-putraḥ* (such as Kakṣivant) or else their names suggested totems, as for instance, Ajigarta or Kaśyapa. Further, that the original seven *gotras* of the *brāhmaṇas* were of mixed Aryan and non-Aryan priests. His analysis of the *gotras* led him into a debate with John Brough.[16] From the study of the *gotras* he went on to the logical point that the language of the Vedic texts could not have been pure Aryan and must have had an admixture of non-Aryan elements reflecting the inclusion of non-Aryans as *brāhmaṇas*. This theory is now more acceptable to those who have worked on Indo-Aryan linguistics, on the basis of the linguistic analyses of the texts and language which clearly indicates non-Aryan structures and forms both in syntax and vocabulary.[17] Kosambi's own use of linguistic analyses bears the stamp of philology and he was evidently less familiar with the changes in linguistic practices of the mid-twentieth century. His etymological reconstruction of Sātakarni as Indo-Austric is an example of this where he makes no attempt to

[14] *ISIH*, p. 174, f.n.1.

[15] 'Early Brahmans and Brahmanism' *JBBRAS*, 1947, XXIII, pp. 39–46; 'On the Origin of the Brahman Gotra,' *JBBRAS*, 1950, XXVI, pp. 21–80. 'Brahman Clans,' *JAOS*, 1953, 73, pp. 202–8.

[16] J. Brough, *The Early Brahmanical System of Gotra and Pravara* (Cambridge, 1953); D.D. Kosambi, 'Brahman Clans' *JAOS*, 1953, 73, pp. 202–8.

[17] T. Burrow, *The Sanskrit Language* (London, 1965); B.M. Emeneau, *Collected Papers*, (Annamalai University, 1967); M.N. Deshpande and P. Hook, *Aryan and non-Aryan in India* (Ann Arbor, 1979).

support his argument by providing other Austric links.[18] The same problem arises with his attempt to equate the Hittite *khatti* with the Sanskrit *kṣatriya* and the Pāli *khettiyo*.[19]

An area in which he successfully utilised his mathematical knowledge was Indian numismatics and more especially in the one coinage system on which he worked in great detail, namely, the punch-marked coins which were in circulation between c. 500-100 BC. These were coins cut from a sheet of silver, each coin bearing a set of symbols but with no legend. Hence their chronology and the agency which issued them was an enigma. Kosambi wished to demonstrate the application of scientific methods for obtaining information from numismatic evidence. He worked initially on a statistical analyses from one hoard with a meticulous weighing of each coin to ascertain loss of weight by wear and tear and with a careful analysis of their fabric and alloy. By arranging the coins in accordance with their weight and their set of symbols he hoped to provide a chronological sequence of the coins and believed that this would in turn provide a clue as to the source of their issue.[20] For the method to be ultimately successful the coins to be used as control had to come from stratified excavations. These could be tested against coins from hoards provided they were free from encrustations. His analyses revealed that the average weight decreases when the symbols on the reverse increase. From this he argued that coins in constant circulation would also be the ones to be weighed and valued more frequently. He maintained that they were originally issued by traders but were ratified by the kings' valuers and marked with the kings' symbols. The next step was the identifying of particular symbols as the marks of particular kings. Whereas the statistical analyses of the coins is generally accepted, the identifications of certain symbols with royalty re-

[18] *ISIH*, pp. 229–30.

[19] *CCAIHO*, p. 77.

[20] 'Study and Methodology of Silver Punch-Marked Coins' *New Indian Antiquary*, 1941, 4, pp. 1–35 and 49–76; 'The Effect of Circulation upon Weight of Metallic Currency,' *Current Science*, 1942, XI, pp. 227–30; *ISIH*, p. 162ff.

main controversial with some numismatists still arguing that the coins may not bear any royal marks. It does seem curious that with major changes in the nature of the state and of royalty during this period, the coins, if connected with royalty, should have remained without any appreciable change in style. It seems implausible that the Mauryan kings would not have issued special coins and would have been content to merely ratify these issued by traders, for, if nothing else they would at least have imitated the Persian and Greek coins which were circulating in West Asia and with which area Indian kings and traders were in contact. It seems more likely that the coins continued to be issued and ratified by guilds as legal tender, a suggestion which has been linked to the occasional legend of *negama* (from *nigama*?) on some issues from Taxila. The evaluation of coins by the king's valuer as described in the *Arthaśāstra* would doubtless have applied to all coins irrespective of where they were issued.

Kosambi's use of archaeology was in part to reconstruct the prehistoric period where he literally walked the stretch around Pune in an effort to record the archaeological data. On the basis of his extensive fieldwork on microlithic sites and through his typology of microlithic artefacts he was able to suggest the routes which herders, pastoralists and incipient traders would have taken across the western Deccan in the pre-historic period.[21] Relating to a more developed culture, he looked for continuities of archaic artefacts and sought to explain these in their fullest function, for example, the function of the saddle-quern which he explained both with reference to those found in archaeological excavations and as well as those in current use.[22] By the term 'use' he meant not merely the technological function but also the role of the object in religious ritual. He was also among the earliest scholars to recognize the significance of the megalithic material and the

[21] 'Pilgrim's Progress: a contribution to the Prehistory of the Western Deccan' in *Myth and Reality*, p. 110ff.

[22] *ISIH*, p. 43ff.

potentialities which it held in the discussion on the origins of many institutions.

Added to the fieldwork was an intelligent understanding of geo-morphology and topography. In many cases his assessment of the historical importance of a site was based on the logic of geography. This he felt should indicate to the historian where to look for sites and the likely nature of the sites. This approach is demonstrated in what can only be called a brilliantly insightful discussion of the trade routes from the west coast upto the plateau and across the *ghats* in the western Deccan.[23] Geographical considerations were partially responsible for the location of urban centres and Buddhist monasteries in this area during the first millennium AD with a continuity of Maratha forts and British railway links in the second millennium.

It was the recognition of cultural survival which led Kosambi to weave so much material from ethnology and anthropology into his historical narrative. This is perhaps best demonstrated in the pages of his *Introduction to the Study of Indian History*, where he describes what he sees in the vicinity of his house in Pune.[24] Here we have history virtually on the door-step, what with the encampment of a nomadic group, the presence of a tribe which had once given rise to a *jāti*, and of another which became a quasi-guild. He noticed trees and sacred groves, stones marking a sacrificial ritual, caves and rock shelters which may have been occupied successively by prehistoric men, by Buddhist monks and later by practitioners of Hindu cults. Such places have a remarkable continuity as sacred centres and often provided a greater historical continuity both in object and ritual than many written texts. These for him were primary areas for archaeological and historical investigation. It is important to clarify that Kosambi was not arguing that religion played a more significant part in Indian culture than has been the case in other cultures, as has been the stand of those who maintain

[23] *Ibid.*, p. 246ff.
[24] *Ibid.*, p. 24ff.

the greater spirituality of the Indian past; but rather, Kosambi's position is that there was a greater survival of the archaic in religious ritual than in other areas of Indian life which speaks of a certain conservatism but at the same time makes it worth investigating historically. This perspective on culture is again demonstrated in the discussion on the probable Harappan religious forms and their continuity into later periods.

Kosambi had little use for physical anthropology. For him, both the measuring of nasal indexes and the theories on the racial identities of India derived therefrom, were worthless.[25] At a wider anthropological level he maintained that one of the clues to understanding the Indian past was the basic factor of the transition from tribe to caste, from small, localized groups to a generalized society.[26] This transition was largely the result of the introduction of plough agriculture in various regions which changed the system of production, broke the structure of tribes and clans and made caste the alternative form of social organization. This process he traced in part from the evolution of clan totems into clan names and then into caste names. The agency through which plough agriculture was introduced would therefore become the major factor of control in caste society. This agency he saw as the brahmanical settlements in various parts of the country. These led to an assimilation of local cults into the brahmanical tradition as is evident from the various *Purāṇas* and *Māhātmyas*. But equally important it led to the sanskritization of local folk cults with the incorporation of *brāhmaṇa* priests and rituals, the association of epic heroes and heroines, and by the inclusion of such cults in Sanskrit mythology.

The interpretation of myths is essential to any study of early cultures and Kosambi's work is peppered with such interpretations. In a detailed discussion of the story of Purūravas and Urvaśi which he traces through its many varients in the texts,[27] he dismis-

[25] *Sovetskaya Etnografia,* Ak. Nauk USSR, No. 1., 1958, pp. 39–57.
[26] *ISIH.*, p. 24ff.
[27] 'Urvaśī and Purūravas' in *Myth and Reality*, p. 42ff.

ses the simplistic nature-myth interpretation of Max Müller and his contemporaries who saw the disappearance of Urvaśi as symbolic of the vanishing dawn on the rising of the sun. Kosambi attempts a functional anthropological analysis in which he argues that it reflects the institution of sacred marriage in prehistoric societies as well as the ritual sacrifice of the hero by the mother goddess.[28] One of the frequent strands in his explanations of myths was related to his belief that societies were matriarchal in origin and many gradually changed to patriliny and that myths therefore reflect the transition from the one to the other. This view was largely derived from the writings of F. Engels[29] and what one might call the 'mother-right school of anthropology.'[30] He applied the same argument to explain the *kumbha* symbol or birth from a jar of certain *brāhmaṇa gotra*s and of the Kauravas in the *Mahābhārata* where the jar has an obvious symbolic equation with the womb. Bride-price is also for him a survival of matriliny.[31] The insistence on a transition from matriarchy to patriliny in every case is not now acceptable since many societies are known to have been patrilineal from the beginning. It is curious that the structural study of myths was known at that time but Kosambi shows little interest in it.

I have tried to indicate the various ways in which Kosambi contributed to Indological studies in his handling of the various sources and data. That his scholarship ranged over a variety of aspects was in conformity with the best Indological tradition which required a many faceted scholar who could claim familiarity with different source materials. What distinguished Kosam-

[28] 'At the Crossroads: a study of mother goddess cult sites,' *Myth and Reality*, p. 82ff.

[29] *The Origin of the Family, Private Property and the State* (London, 1946).

[30] e.g. R. Briffault, *The Mothers* (New York, 1927); O.R. Ehrenfels, *Mother Right in India* (London, 1941).

[31] *ISIH*, p. 27. In his letters to Vidal-Naquet dated 18.9.1965 and 27.9.1965 he provides further examples of this in the wealth paid by Bhīṣma for the marriage of Pāṇḍu to Mādri, the Madra princess, *Mahābhārata* I. 105.1. and also in the form of the marriage of Arjuna to Subhadrā, of the Yadu tribe.

bi from other scholars was that his ultimate concern was with an overall theoretical frame-work, into which, not only was his scattered research directed, but which he propounded as an attempt to comprehend the totality of Indian history. His first book, *An Introduction to the study of Indian History*, drew together the many themes on which he had researched in earlier years and which he had published as papers in various journals of Oriental Studies. This book was to prove his claim not merely to being a historian but to changing the paradigm for early Indian history.

For Kosambi, Marxism provided the clue to understanding the past and he identified his method unambiguously with Marxism. Kosambi would doubtless have accepted the judgement of Jean Paul Sartre that Marxism is the 'necessary' philosophy of our time, by which Sartre meant that even if Marx's particular conclusions are un-acceptable, the method of analysis which he had worked out is virtually unavoidable in the social sciences. Many among the non-Marxist and anti-Marxist historians in this country tried to dismiss the book with the predictable critique of all Marxist histories, that the author was forcing the facts to fit a preconceived theory: a critique which is applied *ad nauseam* to many versions of knowledge which are intellectually uncomfortable for those who are incapable of changing the paradigm and who are fearful of scholars attempting to do so. A few among the more intellectually gifted realized that what Kosambi was doing was not forcing the facts to fit the received Marxist pattern on Indian history, but was instead using a Marxist methodology to investigate a possible pattern and suggest a new framework; that in fact he was using the method creatively. As he himself states elsewhere, Marxism was not being "proved" or "justified", but simply being used as a tool of professional investigation. And this was also part of the reason why he was regarded with suspicion by the then Marxist political establishment in this country, the people whom he has referred to in his writings as the OM—the Official Marxists![32]

[32] In the introduction to *Exasperating Essays* (Poona, 1957), pp. 3–4 and on

Enthusiastic support came to him from intellectuals interested in Marxism and in history and from liberal intellectuals in Europe and America. It is significant that Kosambi was invited to give a series of lectures on the history of Hinduism at London University and to lecture at the Oriental Institute in Moscow in 1955, and this was before any Indian University took such a step.

I would like now to consider his approach to early Indian history with which he was centrally concerned. In the context of his general argument of the transition from tribe to caste, socio-economic formations were his primary interest. He draws his evidence on tribal forms both from literary sources as well as from the survival of such groups into recent centuries and from their interaction with peasant groups. The earliest of such transitions occurred in the Indus valley; hence Kosambi's concern with agrarian technology at that time.[33] He assumed that it was a culture without the plough, that the river bank was cultivated with a harrow and that the seasonal flood water was utilized for irrigation with dams and embankments helping in retaining this water and the river silt for a longer period. The decline of the Indus civilization is attributed to the Aryans who destroyed the agricultural system by breaking the embankments, which action he maintains, is symbolically referred to in the Ṛgvedic descriptions of Indra destroying Vṛtra, and releasing the waters. Kosambi was of the opinion that the plough was brought by the Aryans [i.e. the speakers of Indo-Aryan] who thereby changed agricultural technology. Recent evidence on the Indus civilization makes it clear that plough agriculture was practised even as early as the pre-

p. 18. He says of them, 'These form a decidedly mixed category, indescribable because of the rapidly shifting views and even more rapid political permutations and combinations. The OM included at various times several factions of the CPI, the Congress Socialists, the Royists and numerous left splinter groups . . . The OM Marxism has too often consisted of theological emphasis on the inviolable sanctity of the current party line, or irrelevant quotations from the classics.'

33 *Ibid.*, p. 62ff.

Harappan period and that the plough was known to the non-Aryan since the more commonly used word, for the plough in Vedic literature is of non-Aryan etymology.[34] The theory of the destruction of the embankments is conjectural and may have greater application to dams built to prevent the flooding of the cities rather than for agricultural purposes. Nevertheless the question posed by Kosambi as to why the agrarian base of the Harappan culture declined and was unable to support an urban civilization in the later stages still remains a valid one and is now sought to be answered by evidence of a far reaching ecological change with which Harappan technology could not cope and which eventually resulted in the location of new urban centres in the Ganges valley.

Although he had no use for any theory of an Aryan race, Kosambi did support the idea of the Aryan speaking peoples having settled in north-western India and spreading gradually into the Ganges valley, in both cases initially as conquerors.[35] Such a theory of conquest had been questioned by those working in Indo-Aryan linguistics and it is now being proposed that conquest should be replaced by considering the possibility of migrations and technological changes being responsible for the arrival and the dominance of the Aryan speakers, the resulting long period of co-existence between them and the indigenous peoples being suggested by the evidence of bi-lingualism. Even the archaeological data which was once put forward to support the destruction of the Harappan cities by invaders is now discounted.[36] The new evidence however tends to strengthen the more important point made by Kosambi that much of the Indian tradition from the earliest Vedic texts is already an amalgam of Aryan and non-Aryan as indeed are even those of the highest caste.

Plough agriculture and iron technology when it was intro-

[34] Romila Thapar, 'The Study of Society in Ancient India' in *Ancient Indian Social History: Some Interpretations* (New Delhi, 1978) p. 211ff.

[35] *CCAIHO*, p. 41.

[36] Romila Thapar, *op. cit.*

duced into the Ganges valley led ultimately to the growth of urban centres as well as the recognizable forms of caste. Recent views would include as causal factors in this development, the role of a change in crop patterns with a dependence on rice agriculture, the diversity of irrigation systems, the use of labour in the new technologies and the range of control over these factors by different social groups. This is a fleshing out, as it were, of Kosambi's argument by extending the span of causal factors. Analyses of the structure of caste at this time in terms of the theoretical form given to the actuality, gives further rein to the question implicitly raised by Kosambi, namely, the degree to which ideology and social structure are inter-connected.

The Mauryan monarchy which controlled the Indian sub-continent was a feasible political system according to Kosambi because of the expansion of the village economy through *śūdra* agriculturalists being settled on state lands and by the deportation of prisoners-of-war who were used for the same purpose.[37] He argues against the use of slavery in production in early India and prefers the theory of *śūdra* helotage, although he does not develop this theory in detail. The decline of the Mauryan empire is attributed to an economic crisis, the details of which are debatable. His argument that the currency was debased devolves from his own chronological interpretation of the coins, which as we have seen, is not entirely acceptable, as also the argument that double cropping indicated an economic crisis, for we now know from archaeological sources that double cropping was an established practice even in earlier centuries.[38] However, that the inability of the Mauryan polity to survive must be attributed to causes which in part were certainly economic, cannot be doubted. A more plausible analysis would be to examine the nature of the Mauryan polity in terms of whether the existing man power and agricultural

[37] *ISIH*, p. 176ff.

[38] K.A. Chaudhuri, *Ancient Agriculture and Forestry in Northern India* (Bombay, 1977).

resources were conducive to such a system. Equally important is the question of whether the polity was as centralized as has been made out in historical studies.

Kosambi's treatment of the rise of the Buddhist, Jaina and other sects of that time links them to major technological changes and to urbanism. But above all he maintains that they reflect a situation of detribalization in which they attempt to reach out across castes to a wider social range through their universal ethic. He argues forcefully in support of a mercantile patronage extended to these sects which rooted them in society more firmly than did the help they received from royal patronage. The punch-marked coins are for him an indication of developed commodity production[39] which provided a high status for artisans and traders as members of urban society and their link with religions propagating a universal ethic would not be surprising. This link was demonstrated in his discussion of the post-Maurya period where he examines the role of guilds and artisans as donors to the Buddhist *saṅgha* in the light of the expansion and diffusion of trade. The emergence of occupational *jātis* in urban areas can frequently be associated with this development.

An evident departure from the orthodox Marxist pattern of historical periodization is Kosaṃbi's refusal to apply either the Asiatic Mode of Production or the Slave Mode of Production to early Indian history without modifications of a major kind. For Karl Marx the Indian past conformed, by and large, to what he called the Asiatic Mode of Production characterized by a static society, an absence of private property in land, self-sufficient villages, a lack of a commercial economy and by a state control over the irrigation system. Although he and Engels recognized deviations from this pattern, they saw this pattern as a contrast to that prevalent in Europe and argued that historical stagnancy in India was broken by the coming of colonialism. This was not altogether acceptable to Kosambi, for whom the key to the Indian

[39] *CCAIHO*, p. 125.

past in the advance of plough agriculture over tribal society made a static history impossible. Of the notion of the self-sufficient village economy he writes, '. . . acute and brilliant as these remarks are, they remain misleading nevertheless . . .'.[40] The dependence of the village on external sources for salt and metals would automatically preclude self-sufficiency. Elsewhere he has argued for the existence of the tenant and of the landowning peasant.[41] He did however concede that from the end of the Gupta period there was a relative increase in self-sufficiency and this brought with it a static mode of production which was not the Asiatic mode for it came about during a period of feudalism.[42] He also argued that the lack of a sense of history and the power of myth further reduced individuality. A static mode of production could not have co-existed with a form of feudalism since the latter breeds its own contradictions. Perhaps if he had been questioned on this ambiguity he may have modified his position to argue that the degree of self-sufficiency increased, but not to the extent of the static mode of production becoming the dominant feature.

Elaborating his views on the Asiatic Mode of Production he wrote

> The real difficulty here (not in China) is the misleading documentation. Ancient Indian records derive from the brahman caste and those who read them pay no attention to the function of caste in ancient—(as well as modern and feudal) Indian society. Indian history is, to me, a very fine example of Marxist theory working very well in practice. Unfortunately, Marx had only the solitary report of Buchanan-Hamilton on Karnatak villages, not even the *Foral* of 1640 by the king of Portugal guaranteeing the rights of Goa village communities, which existed in a much more primitive form, and which could not be called 'hydraulic', in view of the torrential rainfall. The Goan organisation (which I have studied elsewhere, *Myth and Reality*, Chapter V) was actually the model for the Karnatak settlement, and survived almost to this day.

[40] *ISIH*, p. 244.
[41] *CCAIHO*, p. 101.
[42] *ISIH*, p. 244ff.

It follows that 'Oriental Despotism' has to be looked at from some other points of view than Wittfogel's hydraulic social aberrations. It seems to me that the two main Marxist considerations are: (1) The incidence of commodity production (per head) with the relative ease of food-gathering. This becomes vital when you consider Africa. By the way, the Pharoah's main function was not regulation of water or irrigation, but distribution of the numerous materials which had all to be imported from a long distance, including wood, metals, and so on. Henri Frankfort has a very neat answer to Toynbee, where he brings this out, in contrast to Mesopotamian development of numerous warring cities. (2) The need to use overriding force to compel the people (in an environment where food-gathering was, however irregular, always possible) to change over to food-production i.e. agriculture with the plough. In Egypt food-gathering was different except in the delta, but the cultivator had to be kept at his work. You will find that the British had to impose a poll-tax in Africa in order to get cheap labour for the mines and the white man's farms.

If you grant this, then it follows that despotism, even of the so-called oriental type, was a tool (however disgusting) used to bring a more productive form of society into existence. But during this very process, there came into being a class of state servants, state nobility or administrators—at times priests, who reduced the need for violence and helped develop the back-lands (as did my own ancestors in Goa and the Buddhist monasteries in China as well as in the Deccan). This class then used the absolute, despotic monarchy and the more or less passive substratum for its own purposes. Hence the changeless appearance of the country, seeing that the actual tools of production need not become more efficient. Under such circumstances, feudalism is a special development used to keep the rule in the hands of a ruling warrior caste-class often conquerors. Don't be misled by the supposed Indian *kshatriya* caste which was oftener than not a brahmanical fiction . . . .[43]

His rejection of the Slave Mode of Production as applicable to the Indian past arose from a hesitation in applying the accepted Marxist periodization of European history. Marx had suggested that primitive communism gave way to a slave mode of production predominant in Greco-Roman antiquity and this in turn gave

[43] Letter to Pierre Vidal-Nàquet dated 4.7.1964.

rise to feudalism in Europe from which evolved the capitalist mode of production. Kosambi was averse to the mechanical application of this model to India as had been done by various historians in Soviet Russia and in India, as for example, by S.A. Dange. Kosambi was caustic in his evaluation of Dange's book, *From Primitive Communism to Slavery*, which he said followed the Russian analysis and which analysis, '. . . saves a certain type of "left intellectual" the trouble of reading anything else or thinking for himself.'[44] Kosambi's analysis differed from any existing model. He maintains that the statement of the Greek ambassador Megasthenes (of the fourth century BC) that there was an absence of slavery in India was correct because Megasthenes makes a comparison with Sparta which suggests helots instead of slaves.[45] Kosambi states that at this period the *śūdra*s were essentially helots. He does not however discuss in greater detail the nature of *śūdra* helotage. Whereas the origin of the *śūdra* caste could perhaps be traced to a form of helotage, the classification cannot hold for the entire past. At the ideological level it would be clearly contradicted by the early *Dharmaśāstra* exposition of the *varṇa* theory where the origin of the *śūdra* is attributed to mixed caste marriages including those involving the upper castes. Such a theory even if not based on actuality would have undermined the notion of helotage. The possibility of a Slave Mode of Production in early India is problematical since it is difficult to assess the ratio of slaves to other forms of labouring men nor is there a clear distinction between slaves in domestic employ or in agricultural and craft production. Doubtless these numbers would also have varied in the *gaṇasaṅgha* chiefships where they were probably higher and in the kingdoms where with a diversity of labour, slavery for production may have been smaller. It would also be important to consider

[44] *Ibid.*, p. 6; see also, 'Marxism and Ancient Indian Culture'. *ABORI*, 1949, 29, pp. 271–77. Kosambi's views on his relations with the Communist Party of India over his review of Dange's book and his relations with Dange are described in his letters to Vidal Naquet dated 22.11.1963 and 4.12.1963.

[45] *ISIH*, p. 187.

the degree of unfreedom of the *dāsa* in relation to the *karmakāra, bhṛitaka* and *śūdra* which would involve questions of the legal status of these categories.

The Feudal Mode of Production Kosambi accepts as relevant to pre-modern Indian history, although even here he makes his own distinction between what he calls, 'feudalism from above' and 'feudalism from below', and which he regards as the peculiar features of Indian feudalism. Feudalism from above was his characterization of the changes which came about in the late first millennium AD subsequent to the Gupta period.[46] Incidentally he has little time for the Gupta period and is justifiably contemptuous of the nationalist historians who described it as the golden age of Hindu revivalism. His contempt is summed up in the sentence, 'Far from the Guptas reviving nationalism, it was nationalism that revived the Guptas.'[47] Recent research has not only tarnished some of the golden quality of this age, but has on occasion even revealed that a part of it was mere tinsel. The changes noticeable in the post-Gupta period were mainly those of an increase in the granting of land with a greater frequency of transition from tribe to caste through the introduction of plough agriculture, a decline in trade and commodity production which adversely affected the growth of urban centres, the decentralization of the army and a concentration of wealth at local courts. With this was associated the spread of *bhakti* cults whose emphasis on loyalty and devotion he saw as a characteristic feature of feudal society. In a discussion on private property in land, central to the concept of the Asiatic Mode of Production, he argues that it should be viewed in the Indian context which implies, firstly, that actual cultivators were ex-tribals who still regarded land as territory deriving from kinship rights, and secondly, the holding of a field was proof of membership of community rather than ownership of land and thirdly, that is a non-commodity producing village or one located near waste

[46] *Ibid.*, p. 275.

[47] *Ibid.*, p. 291.

land, land would have no sale value. The only conditions were the regular payment of taxes to either the grantee or the king. These arguments read more like an attempt to somehow salvage the notion of the absence of private property without a willingness to admit the pattern of the Asiatic Mode of Production as an explanatory model. Nor are these arguments wholly convincing because although in some areas the cultivators were recent converts to peasantry in others they were peasants of long standing since many of the grants of land were made in villages of well-established cultivators. The statement that land had no sale value in newly settled areas is contradicted by inscriptional evidence in some areas where, in Bengal for example, land is sold and the price is stated in districts which were regarded as being on the edge of waste land.[48] Part of the problem with his analysis of the two phases of feudalism, and this is a problem of which he is well aware, is that no generalization can cover the entire sub-continent since the changes varied from region to region.[49]

In his discussion on feudalism from below he draws his evidence mainly from Kashmir and Rajasthan and depicts a more clearly recognizable form of feudalism but with specific Indian features.[50] This phase is characterized by political decentralization accompanied by a low level of technology with production for the household and the village and not for a market, and the holding of land by lords on a service tenure who also have judicial or quasi-judicial functions in relation to the dependent population. The Indian features were the absence of demesne farming on the lord's estate by forced labour where in many cases, slaves were used instead, leading to an increase in slaves; there was also an absence of guilds and of any organized church. The backwardness of technology allowed of an easy conquest of northern India by those with a more advanced military technology. Changes in the

[48] B. Morrison, *Political Centres and Culture Regions in Early Bengal* (Tucson, 1970).
[49] *CCAIHO*, p. 177ff.
[50] *ISIH*, p. 326ff.

ruling class did not substantially affect the nature of feudalism in India and it continued until the coming of colonialism.

Kosambi's definition of feudalism would today find its critics as also would its general applicability to the sub-continent be debated. On the latter point one would have to consider whether other systems prevalent in other parts of the sub-continent would seriously subtract from the generalization.[51] The nature of control over land was different in parts of the peninsula as also was the condition of trade, where the rise of powerful guilds was characteristic of this period. The increase in the number of slaves was not such as to constitute a Slave Mode of Production and as Kosambi maintains quite correctly there was no slave economy of the Roman kind to initiate the institution of the manor. The existence of serfdom has also been suggested for many areas. Although there was no organized church nevertheless there is what Max Weber has called 'monastic landlordism' both among Buddhist and Hindu sects, which at some levels was a parallel system to that of church lands in Europe. The monastic centres of this period were opulent and powerful. Kosambi argues that religious sects frequently failed to provide the ethical and religious values by which they had once held the society, but he does not consider the monastic institution as the foci of political and economic control, a role which it often played at this time.[52]

It is curious that Kosambi takes as his model feudalism in England and shows no familiarity with the classic work on feudal society by Marc Bloch which would have been far more pertinent to his analyses. (His facility in French would have enabled him to have read Marc Bloch in the original). In a sense, this points to something of a narrowness in his wider historical reading. Although far from being an orthodox Marxist he nevertheless showed little interest in schools of analyses other than the Marxist

[51] R.S. Sharma had argued for a substantial similarity in many parts of northern India, *Indian Feudalism* (Calcutta, 1965).

[52] An example of the analysis of this role can be found in H. Kulke, *Jagannātha Kult und Gajapati Königtam* (Weisbaden, 1979).

as far as interpreting early societies was concerned. He does not for example indicate any familiarity with the works of those who were critical of Lewis Morgan and Frederick Engels inspite of using Marxist analyses as a starting point for the study of early societies, such as Karl Polyani. It is also curious that inspite of his interest in French scholarship (arising out of a concern with French colonial activities in Vietnam and North Africa) he was not introduced to the writings of French historians such as Fernand Braudel with which, one suspects, he would have found a rapport. Whereas his respect for the works of Gordon Childe and George Thomson is evident in his own studies, his acquaintance with Moses Finley's work on the Greeks came later[53] and one wonders whether he would have analysed the Indian epics in a manner similar to Finley's analysis of the Greek epics. Convinced as he was of the correctness of one methodology, Kosambi seems to have found the debate on methodology unnecessary. His utilization of Indian anthropological literature was more as a source of ethnology and a study of survivals and indigenous forms rather than as a means of examining the validity of any anthropological method. Possibly this limitation may also have been due to the tendency among Indian Marxists at that time to confine themselves to the writings of British Marxists, which can perhaps be explained as a curious reflection on the limitations of colonial scholarship where, even in radical circles the intellectual metropolis remained British with occasional forays into the writings of Soviet scholars. This is in striking contrast to more recent years in which the translations of European Marxist writing and that from other parts of the world are as widely read as the works of British Marxists.[54] A more

[53] M. Finley, *The World of Odysseus,* was first published in 1954. The fact that he was initially working in the United States would at that time have made his books less easily available in India. Kosambi refers to his study *Ancient Greeks* as being most stimulating, rather than to his more acclaimed work on the Greek epics.

[54] The easy availability of English translations has helped in this, such translations resulting mainly from the interest in Neo-Marxism on the part

mundane explanation may be the paucity of new books at that time and Kosambi was very conscious of this lack of availability of up-to-date research. In his personal correspondence with scholars in fields other than Indology he makes repeated requests to be kept informed of new studies since such information was not available in India. Where he could obtain such works he read them with great thoroughness and commented at length on them, as for example, on Maurice Godelier's views on early societies, many of which views he endorsed. That the deepest intellectual influence on Kosambi came from the writings of Frederick Engels is evident from both his books on Indian history.[55]

Such limitations, as these may be, are marginal to the serious quality of Kosambi's work, a quality which is enhanced by the intellectual honesty with which he justifies his use of Marxist methodolgy. His was a mind which by any standards would be considered outstanding. He combined in himself the best of a rigorous Indian intellectual tradition and rejected the facile revivalism and cultural chauvinism which in recent decades have emasculated Indian thinking. In changing the paradigm Kosambi presented a view of Indian history which sought answers to the fundamental questions of how and why Indian society is what it is today. He provided a new theoretical framework which was not a mechanical application of theories derived from elsewhere but was hammered out by his proficiency in handling a variety of sources and the intellectual perceptions and originality of thought

---

of American radicals and academics. It is significant that some of the most stimulating debates on precapitalist societies emanating from new Marxist writing are to be found in the issues of the last fifteen years of *Current Anthropology* and *American Anthropologist*.

55 A view put forward in the course of a conversation by Charles Malamoud (who translated *CCAIHO* into French) and with which view I am in agreement. In a letter to Vidal-Naquet dated 4.6.1964 Kosambi writes, 'I learned from these two great men [Marx and Engels] what questions to ask and then went to fieldwork to find the answers, because the material did not exist in published books.'

which he brought to bear on his explanations. Fresh evidence may well lead to a reconsideration of the answers which he gave to these questions but his questions and his concerns still remain valid. Even in this reconsideration we are often dependent on the leads which he initially gave and which he indicated were worth pursuing. Kosambi raised the debate on early Indian history from variations in narrative to contending theoretical formulations.

Above all he was concerned with the contemporary relevance of his understanding of the past. But he insisted that the relevance was never to serve any doctrinaire purpose;[56] rather, it should stem from what he thought was the natural function of the historian. I can only conclude with what he himself quoted as the summation of the role of the historian. E.H. Carr writes: 'The function of the historian is neither to love the past nor to emancipate himself from the past, but to master and understand it as the key to the understanding of the present. Great history is written precisely when the historian's vision of the past is illuminated by insight into problems of the present . . . . The function of history is to promote a profounder understanding of both past and present through the inter-relation between them.'[57]

[56] *CCAIHO*, p. 24.
[57] *What is History*? pp. 20, 31, 62.

Early India: an Overview

The scope of ancient Indian history is undergoing some modification and the erstwhile ancient period, which stretched from Harappan times to the early second millennium AD is now being sub-divided into the ancient and the early medieval period. The nomenclature 'early medieval' does little towards either explaining itself or the subsequent medieval period: but the differentiation between pre-Gupta and post-Gupta history is a necessary and welcome change as also is the continuity between the late first millennium and the second millennium AD.

Harappan society remains enigmatic. There have been few attempts at detailed reconstruction from the archaeological evidence. This is in part because the variety of data required from studies such as palaeo-botany, ecology and hydrology remains limited for such a reconstruction and partially also because there are few archaeologists working on India willing to attempt a theoretical reconstruction in which the use of concepts from other disciplines such as anthropology, demography and statistics would be a prerequisite.[1] Such a reconstruction is especially re-

[1] An exception to this is the recent study of Harappan and West Asian trade by Shereen Ratnagar, *Encounters: The Westerly Trade of the Harappan Civilisation* (Delhi, 1981). A primary requirement relating to ecology and hydrology would be a series of studies along the lines of those Robert Mac Adams on Mesopotamia, particularly *The Heartland of Cities* (Chicago, 1981). Evidence from other disciplines can be utilized more effectively through a larger input of scientific techniques into excavation and analyses

quired with the fading of the so-called 'dark age' between the Harappa Culture and subsequent societies.[2] The question as to how far Vedic society is entirely Indo-Aryan or draws on the Harappan tradition in language, ritual and institutions becomes even more apposite than before.[3]

It is in the study of the many sub-periods within the broad boundaries of the ancient period that fundamental questions arise, providing scope for wide-ranging discussion. For a better definition of these sub-periods and in the interests of historical clarity a considerable refining of concepts and theories becomes necessary. Many of the crucial terms used in the definitions have been ap-

---

as well as data gathered from such disciplines. This may well happen in the near future now that archaeology the world over is drawing increasingly on scientific sources and less on the study of the classics. This calls for a little more theoretical daring on the part of archaeologists working on India and a concern with questions relating to the nature of Harappan society. The decipherment of the Harappa script, still a long way off, would of course be a help and would involve using the more conventional techniques of linguistics and cultural symbols. But the reconstruction of Harappan society could be met half-way by an approach which tries to intelligently reconstitute the society on the basis of material remains, environment and ecology. That the interest in ecology and environment does not have a relevance limited to archaeological data alone is clear from the recent Harris-versus-Heston debate on why the cow is sacred in India. M. Harris, 'The Cultural Ecology of India's Sacred Cattle,' *Current Anthropology*, 1966, 7, pp. 51–60; A. Heston, 'An Approach to the Sacred cow of India,' *Current Anthropology*, 1971, 12, pp. 191–209; S. Odend'hal, 'Energetics of Indian Cattle in their Environment,' *Human Ecology*, 1973, I.I. pp. 3–22.

[2] Archaeological continuities are being discovered between Harappan and post-Harappan societies as for example, in the repeated occurence of the Black-and-red Ware from Harappan to proto-historic times and more recently the overlap in the Punjab between Late Harappan and the Painted Grey Ware culture (associated by some with Vedic society) J.P. Joshi and Madhubala, 'Life During the Period of Overlap of Late Harappan and PGW Cultures,' *Journal of the Indian Society of Oriental Art*, 1977–78, NS, IX, pp. 20–9.

[3] Romila Thapar, 'The Archaeology of the Agnicayana,' in F. Staal, ed., *AGNI—The Vedic Ritual of the Fire Altar*, vol. I (Berkeley, 1982).

plied to such diverse social forms that they cease to have a specific meaning and tend to mask the diversities. This sharpening of focus becomes particularly necessary with the growing interest in social and economic history. It will also help in understanding the process of historical mutation over time. Although there is now a rich literature describing segments of the period, the explanation of change from one to the next and the linkages between these require a fuller consideration. A creatively critical discussion is called for on the terms used to translate categories mentioned in the sources since much of the interpretation depends on such discussion.

The nineteenth century was the age of the grand edifices of historical explanation and theoretical construction. While some of these edifices still stand firm, others are tottering. Even those which still stand often require repair and renovation, sometimes of a structural kind, in the light of new knowledge and fresh theories. The refining of concepts and theories therefore becomes a necessary part of the historical exercise and is particularly incumbent on those who, as conscientous historians, build their explanations on the basis of theoretical frameworks.[4] It is of this need for the refining of concepts that I would like to speak.[5]

Among the early sub-periods, Vedic society has been de-

[4] In the refining of concepts and theories the comparative method can be a useful tool. This involves an awareness of the historical analyses of other cultures and the use of specific categories of explanation which may not be directly applicable to early Indian history, but which would nevertheless generate questions and comparisons which can in turn assist in fresh analysis. It is to be deeply regretted that serious expertise on the ancient history of areas outside the Indian sub-continent is generally unavailable in Indian centres of research.

[5] I have elsewhere analysed in greater detail some of the themes which I am touching upon here. Questions relating to lineage-based societies, the sacrificial ritual and the peasant economy were considered by me in *From Lineage to State.* A summary of these ideas was contained in a paper, 'State Formation in Early India, *International Social Science Journal,* 1980, XXXII, No. 4, pp. 655–669.

scribed as tribal. The term 'tribal', which we have all used in the past, has rightly come in for some questioning.[6] In its precise meaning it refers to a community of people claiming descent from a common ancestor. In its application however, it has been used to cover a variety of social and economic forms, not to mention claims to biological and racial identities; and this tends to confuse the original meaning. Even as a convention it has lost much of its precision. The more recently preferred term, lineage, narrows the focus. Although the economic range remains, lineage does emphasize succession and descent with the implication that these are decisive in determining social status and control over economic resources. It also helps differentiate between chiefships where lineage dominates and kingship, which as a different category, evokes a larger number of impersonal sanctions. The concept of *vaṃśa* (succession) carries a meaning similar to lineage and is central to Vedic society with its emphasis on succession even as a simulated lineage. Thus *vaṃśa* is used to mean lineage or descent group among the *rājanya*s and *kṣatriya*s but is also used in the list of Upaniṣadic teachers where succession does not appear to be by birth but by the passing on of a tradition of knowledge.[7] Lineage also becomes important in the structure of each *varṇa*, defined by permitted rules of marriage and kinship and by ranking in an order of status, the control over resources being implicit. In this sense the emergence of the four *varṇas* is closely allied to the notions of a lineage-based society.[8]

In a stratified society the reinforcing of status is necessary. But where there is no recognized private property in land and no effective state such reinforcing has to be done by sanctions which often take a ritual or religious form. In the absence of taxation as a system of control in the Vedic period, sacrificial ritual functioned as the occasion for renewing the status of the *yajamāna*, initially a

[6] M.H. Fried, *The Notion of Tribe* (Menlo Park, 1975).
[7] *Bṛhadāranyaka Upaniṣad*, II. 6. 1ff; IV. 6. 1ff; VI. 5. 1ff.
[8] Romila Thapar, *From Lineage to State*, pp. 37–69.

rājanya or a *kṣatriya*. Apart from its religious and social role sacrificial ritual also had an economic function. It was the occasion when wealth which had been channelled to the *yajamāna* was distributed by him in the form of gifts to the *brāhmaṇa* priests which strengthened their social rank and ensured them wealth. The ritual served to restrict the distribution of wealth to the *brāhmaṇa*s and the *kṣatriya*s but at the same time prevented a substantial accumulation of wealth by either, for whatever came in the form of gifts and prestations from the lesser clans, the *viś*, to the ruling clans, the *kṣatriyas*, was largely consumed in the ritual and the remainder gifted to the *brāhmaṇa*s. Generosity being important to the office of the chief, wealth was not hoarded. The display, consumption and distribution of wealth at the major rituals such as the *rājasūya* and the *aśvamedha,* was in turn a stimulus to production, for the ritual was also seen as a communication with and sanction from the supernatural. Embedded in the sacrificial ritual therefore were important facets of the economy. This may be a partial explanation of why a major change to the state system and a peasant economy occurred initially in the mid-first millennium BC not in the western Ganga valley but in the adjoining area of the middle Ganga valley. This change was occasioned not only by an increase in economic production and a greater social disparity but also by the fact that the prestation economy associated with the lineage-based society became more and more marginal in the latter region and in some areas was altogether absent.

The term 'peasant economy' is frowned upon by some scholars as an imprecise concept.[9] However it is of some use as a measurement of change. The label of 'peasant' has been applied to a variety of categories some of which are dissimilar. The use of a

[9] J. Ennew *et al.*, 'Peasantry as an Economic Category,' *Journal of Peasant Studies*, 1977, IV, 4, pp. 295–322; M. Harrison, 'The Peasant Mode of Production in the work of A. V. Chayanov,' *Journal of Peasant Studies*, 1977, IV, 4, pp. 323–36; Utsa Patnaik, 'Neo-Populism and Marxism: The Chayanovian View of the Agrarian Question and its Fundamental Fallacy,' *Journal of Peasant Studies*, 1979, VI, 4, pp. 375–420.

single word as a portmanteau description confuses the categories and therefore a differentiation is necessary. Eric Wolf at one point defines peasants as:

> . . . rural cultivators whose surpluses are transferred to a dominant group of rulers that uses the surpluses both to underwrite its own standard of living and to distribute the remainder to groups in society that do not farm but must be fed for their specific goods and services in turn.[10]

This definition seems to me inadequate even in terms of Wolf's study of peasants, for the important point is not merely the existence of a surplus but the mechanism by which it is transferred and it is to this that I would relate the emergence of a peasant economy. That the recognition of an incipient peasant economy in various parts of India is significant to the study of social history hardly needs stressing, since, concomitant with this is also the establishing of particular kinds of state systems, varient forms of *jātis* and new religious and cultural idioms in the area.

For the early period of Indian history the term peasant has been used to translate both the Ṛgvedic *viś*[11] as well as the *gahapati* of Pāli sources. But some distinction is called for. The Vedic *viś* was primarily a member of a clan although this did not preclude him from being a cultivator as well. The transferring of surpluses, in this case the voluntary prestations of the *viś* to the *kṣatriya*, points to a stratified rather than an egalitarian society and the simile of the *kṣatriya* eating the *viś* like the deer eating the grain[12] would indicate greater pressures for larger prestations. But the transfer was not through an enforced system of taxation. In the absence of private ownership of land, the relationship of the *viś* to the *kṣatriya* would have been less contrapuntal with little need of an

[10] E. Wolf, *Peasants* (New Jersey, 1966), pp. 3–4.

[11] This was popularized through A.A. Macdonell and A.B. Keith's *Vedic Index of Names and Subjects*, 1912. The technical term for the cultivator was *kīnāśa* and the root *kṛṣ* is used more frequently in association with cultivation.

[12] *Śatapatha Brāhmaṇa*, VIII. 7.1.2; VIII. 7.2.2; IX. 4,3,5.

enforced collection of the surplus. The context of Vedic references to *bali, bhāga* and *śulka* (the terms used in later periods for taxes) suggest that they were voluntary and random although the randomness gradually changed to required prestations, particularly at sacrificial rituals. However the three major prerequisites governing a system of taxation—a contracted amount, collected at stipulated periods by persons designated as tax collectors—are absent in the Vedic texts. The recognition of these prerequisites in the post-Vedic period and the collection of taxes from the cultivators by the state would seem decisive in registering the change from cultivators to peasants in which the existence of an economy based on peasant agriculture becomes clear.

The introduction of taxation presupposes the impersonal authority of the state and some degree of alienation of the cultivator from the authority to whom the surplus is given, unlike the lineage-based society where prestations are more personalized. Taxation reduced the quantity of prestations and became the more substantial part of what was taken from the peasant, but prestations were not terminated. The sanction of the religious ritual becomes more marginal and that of the state more central, the change occurring gradually over time. The formation of the state is therefore tied into this change. For the cultivator land becomes property or a legal entity and the pressures on cultivation have to do not only with subsistance but also with a provision for ensuring a surplus. This highlights the difference between appropriation in the earlier system and exploitation in the latter.

The Vedic *viś* was more a generalized term in which herding, cultivation and minimal crafts adequate to a household were included. Such groups were germane to the later peasant household. In effect, because the relationship with the dominant *kṣatriya* was based on gifts and prestations rather than on taxes, these cultivators would seem part of a lineage society in which their subservience to a dominant group arises more out of the exigencies of kinship or the ordering of clans than out of exploited labour, although the latter can be seen to increase in time.

The gradual mutation which took place becomes evident from the frequent references in the Pāli sources to the *gahapati*. The existence of the *gahapati* focuses more sharply on the presence of what might be called a peasant economy. But to translate *gahapati* as peasant is to provide a mere slice of its total meaning. Derived from *gṛhapati*, the head of the household, the term *gahapati* includes a range of meanings such as, the wealthy *mahāśālā-brāhamaṇas* addressed as *gahapatis* by the Buddha,[13] who had received as donations extensive, tax-free, arable land as well as those who paid taxes—the wealthy land-owners who cultivated their large farms with the help of slaves and hired labourers (*dāsa-bhṛtaka*).[14] Those at the lower end of the scale who either owned small plots of land or were professional ploughmen are more often referred to as the *kassakas*.[15] An intermediate group is also implied in one of the *Dharmaśūtras*.[16] The *Arthaśāstra* mentions tenants as *upavāsa* and also refers to another category, the *śūdra* cultivators settled by the state on cultivable or waste land on a different system of tenure from the above; as also the range of cultivators employed on the state farms supervised by the overseers of agriculture, the *sītādhyakṣa*.[17]

Gahapati with reference to agrarian society, therefore, is perhaps better translated as the landowner of some substance who would generally pay taxes to the state except when the land which he owned was a religious benefice. Private land ownership and

[13] e.g. *Majjhima Nikāya*, I. 401.

[14] As for example the *gahapati* Meṇḍaka, *Mahāvagga*, VI. 34.

[15] *Dīgha Nikāya*, I. 61; *Saṁyukta Nikāya*, I.172; III. 155; IV. 314; *Aṅguttara Nikāya*, I. 241; 229; 239.

[16] The *Baudhāyana Dharmasūtra* III. 2. 1–4 refers to householders of the upper *varṇa*s who can in some cases be tenants and who cultivate six *nivartana*s (*bīghās*) of land. These were not poor peasants for they are also described as *śālina*, living in well-to-do homes, and would probably constitute an intermediary category between the *gahapati* and the *kassaka*. That this was a recognized category seems evident from their mode of subsistance being described as *ṣannivartana* (six *nivartana*s).

[17] III. 10.8; II. 1.1.

the payment of taxes demarcates this period as one in which a peasant-based economy is evident. Traces of the lineage based society continued in the marking of status by *varṇa* and the performance, although by now of marginal economic significance, of the sacrificial rituals.

That the *gahapati* was not even just a landowner but more a man of means is supported by the fact that it was from the ranks of the *gahapatis* that there emerged the *seṭṭhis* or financiers.[18] The two terms are often associated in the literature and this is further attested in the votive inscriptions recording donations to the *sangha* in central India and the western and eastern Deccan from the late first millennium BC.[19] *Gahapati* fathers have *seṭṭhi* sons as well as the other way round. It would seem that *gahapati* status was acquired through the practice of any respectable profession which provided a decent income, although the most frequent references are to land-ownership and commerce.

This is not to suggest that trade originated with the land-owning groups but rather that the large-scale commercialiaztion of exchange was tied to the emergence of the *gahapati*. In examining the origins of trade it is necessary to define more clearly the nature of the exchange involved. Broadly, there are some recognizable forms of exchange which can either develop into commercialized exchange or supplement it. There is evidence of luxury goods exchanged by ruling groups as a part of gift-exchange. Marriage alliances between *kṣatriya* families involved an exchange of gifts. Thus when Bharata visits his maternal kinsmen, he returns with gifts.[20] This is not an exchange based on need but is a channel

[18] *Aṅguttara Nikāya* IV. 282; VIII. 1.16.

[19] *Epigraphia Indica*, X. 1909–10. Lüders List Nos: 1056, 1062, 1073, 1075, 1121, 1127, 1209, 1281, etc. The inscriptions are later than the Pāli texts and may indicate the repetition of a process which had occurred earlier in the Gaṅgā valley.

[20] *Rāmāyaṇa* VII. 90. 1–5. Among the gifts were horses, probably imported from Gandhāra which was close enough to the Kekeya territory. The trade in horses from the north-west would doubtless have been accelerated by

through which status and kinship is confirmed. It may in addition lead to other forms of exchange. The major royal sacrifices required tributes and gifts and the *rājasūya* of Yudhiṣṭhira provides an interesting inventory of valued items.[21] The more ordinary sacrificial rituals involved the giving of gifts such as cattle, horses, gold, *dāsi*s and chariots by the *yajamāna* to the priests.[22] These gifts became part of a distribution and exchange of wealth which in the lineage based societies formed the salient part of the wealth of those who ruled, whereas in the change to an economy based on peasant agriculture, they were merely a part of the wealth accumulated by the ruling families and the more wealthy *gahapatis*.

Less spectacular but more essential was another form of exchange, that of raw materials and commodities brought by itinerant groups such as smiths and pastoralists. It has been argued that the itinerant metal smiths formed a network of connections between villages.[23] Metal, particularly iron, was also a major item of regular trade. The role of pastoralists in trading circuits is now coming in for considerable attention particularly with reference to those groups which had a regular pattern of transhumance.[24] Exchange through sources of itinerant professionals was probably

forms of exchange. Romila Thapar, 'The *Rāmāyaṇa*: theme and variation,' in S.N. Mukherjee, ed., *India History and Thought* (Calcutta, 1982), pp. 221–53.

[21] *Mahābhārata*, Sabhā Parvan, 47.5; Romila Thapar, 'Some Aspects of the Economic Data in the Mahābhārata, *ABORI* (Poona, 1977–78), LIX, pp. 993–1007; 'The Historian and the Epic,' *ABORI*, 1979, LX, pp. 199–213.

[22] Romila Thapar, '*Dāna* and *dakṣinā* as forms of exchange,' *Ancient Indian Social History : Some Interpretations*, p. 105ff.

[23] D.D. Kosambi, *Introduction to the Study of Indian History*, Bombay, 1956. pp. 11, 91.

[24] Apart from the question of whether or not the Ṛgvedic Aryan speakers introduced iron technology to northern India, it would be worth examining whether as pastoralists there were patterns of movement which permitted them to maintain a symbiotic relationship with pre-existing agricultural communities. This would perhaps explain the factor of bi-lingualism in Vedic Sanskrit.

the starting point of the beat of pedlars which is a continuing feature of one level of exchange in India.

Yet another category is what might be called exchange between one settlement and the next. This is a useful basis for plotting the gradual diffusion of an item, as for example, the better quality varieties of pottery from excavations. Such an exchange provides evidence not only on local trade but also on the geographical reach of intra-regional contacts. Some of these settlements may then have come to play the role of local markets, the equivalent perhaps of what the Pāli texts refer to as *nigama*. These in turn are likely to have been the nuclei of urban growth as in the case of Rājagṛha and Śrāvastī.[25]

Distinct from all these is the familiar picture of trade which dominates the scene in the post-Mauryan period. This is the commercial exchange between two or more centres processing and producing commodities specifically destined for trade. The organization of this more complex form involved a hierarchy of producers and traders some of whom were sedentary while others were carriers of the items traded but of a different order from pedlars and pastoralists. The picture of commercialized exchange emerges from Buddhist texts and by the time of the *Arthaśāstra*, it is regarded as a legitimate source of revenue for the state. The question then arose of the degree of state interference and control which would be conducive to increasing the finances of the state.[26] The major artefact in this trade (other than the commodities) is coined metallic money, providing evidence of the degree of complexity and the extent of such trade and trading circuits. These early coins in some instances were issued by the *nigama* and in other cases may have been issued by local authorities or possibly by ruling families. In the post-Mauryan period dynastic issues gain currency, a clear pointer to the importance of commercialized exchange. However even in this period local issues remain in circulation suggesting multiple levels of exchange.

[25] N. Wagle, *Society at the Time of the Buddha* (Bombay, 1966), p. 22.
[26] *Arthaśāstra* IV. 2.

With such commercialized exchange the control of trade routes becomes a significant factor in political policy and military annexations. A recent analysis of the Silk Trade, involving a variety of levels of exchange from gift-exchange to sophisticated emporia, in the context of political relations between tribal groups and established centres of political power, suggests ways in which the complicated question of trade, often treated as a uniform monolith by historians of ancient India, may be investigated.[27] The trade of the Roman empire with India, as is clear from both commodities and the function of money, also spans a similar range. Diverse forms of exchange suggest the coexistence of various economic levels within larger trading systems and sharpen the social contours of the groups involved.

The analysis of trade also requires locating those involved in these exchanges in the social hierarchy of the time. In the production of goods for exchange, artisans, whether individuals or in guilds, relate to merchants and financiers in forms as diverse as the various categories of cultivators to land-owners. The role of the *śilpin* (artisan) and the *śreṇī* (guild) is quite distinct from the *seṭṭhi*. Their presence registers a change in the nature of the trade as also does the differentiation between categories of professionals such as the *vānija*, the *seṭṭhi* and the *sārthavāha*. Clearly there is a sea change when commercialized exchange becomes active. The investment required for an elaborate trade can only be provided

[27] M.C. Raschke, 'New Studies in Roman Commerce with the East,' in H. Temporim and W. Haase, eds., *Aufsteig und Niedergang der Romischen Welt* (Berlin, 1978). The Silk Trade spanning Central Asia, northern India and the eastern Mediterranean drew on a variety of exchange systems and Raschke's discussion on the role of silk as part of the exchange of gifts in Central Asia provides a new perspective on that section of the trade. An almost graphic representation of the varieties of exchange comes from the recent discoveries of rock engravings and inscriptions, the latter from the Kuṣāna period onwards along the Karakorum Highway in Gilgit. K. Jettmar, *Rock Carvings and Inscriptions in the Northern areas of Pakistan* (Islamabad, 1982); A.H. Dani, *Chilas* (Islamabad, 1983).

by a well-endowed social group which can invest its surplus in risk-taking ventures. The obvious category was the *gahapati* who could fall back on land if the venture failed. That it turned out to be highly successful is clear from the fact that not only did the *seṭṭhi*s emerge from the ranks of the *gahapati*s, but, by the post-Mauryan period, had an independent identity as financiers and gradually superceded the *gahapati*s.[28] The wealth of the *seṭṭhi*s became in turn an avenue to power, for some of them were known to be the financiers of kings and obtained in return rights to collect revenue, perhaps the proto-type of what was later to become the regular form of emoluments to administrative officers.[29] On the manifestations of trade, Buddhist and Jaina sources together with epigraphic and archaeological evidence provide a useful counter-point to the *Dharmaśāstra* literature.

The link between agriculture and commerce is important for understanding the changes in the subsequent period. The opulence of those involved in commerce was poured into the adornment of religious monuments, monasteries and images and in the conspicuous consumption which is associated with the wealthier towndwellers of these times. This tends to obscure the agrarian scene where one notices less of *mahāśālā* landowners and large estates and more of those with small holdings. Small plots of land could be purchased and donated to religious beneficiaries and it seems unlikely, as has been argued, that such sales were restricted to religious donations.[30] Smallholdings together with the alienation of land could point to some degree of impoverishment among peasants. The inclusion of debt bondage (*āhitaka* and *ātmavikreta*) as a regular if not frequent category of slavery,[31] as well as the increasing references to *viṣṭi* (forced labour or a labour tax), sug

[28] I. Fiser, 'The Problem of the Seṭṭhi in Buddhist Jātakas,' *Archiv Orienta[l]* (Prague, 1954), XXII, pp. 238–66.

[29] *Ibid.*, p. 261.

[30] The *Arthaśāstra* refers clearly to the sale of land. II. 1.7; III. 9.3, 15–1[7]; III. 10.9.

[31] *Arthaśāstra* III. 2.; Nārada I. 128; V. 29; Manu XI. 59.

gest a different rural scene from that of the preceding period. That oppressive taxation had become a recognized evil is explicitly mentioned in various texts.[32]

This mutation was endemic to the evident change in the post-Gupta period. Where trade flourished there the resources of the urban centres and the trade routes bouyed up the system; but this period points to a declining trade in many areas.[33] Internal commercialized trade requires the ballast of agrarian settlements and where lineage based societies could be converted into peasant economies there the agrarian support to trade would be strengthened. Earlier networks of exchange had permitted an easier co-existence with lineage based societies. Their resources, generally raw materials such as timber and gem-stones could, as items of exchange, be easily tapped by traders through barter and direct exchange without disturbing the social structure to any appreciable degree. On the other hand because of the requirement of land and labour, state systems more heavily dependent on a peasant economy had to absorb these societies and convert them into peasant economies in order to extract the benefits. Where trade declined or where new states were established the need to develop the agrarian economy became urgent. The granting of land appears to have been the mechanism adopted for changing the agrarian situation. The reasons for this change in the post-Gupta period need more detailed investigation particularly at a regional level.[34] In the very useful work done so far substantial

[32] *Viṣṇu Purāṇa* IV. 24; *Mahāsupina Jātaka* No. 77; *Mahābhārata* Aranyaka Parvan 188.18ff; Śānti Parvan 254. 39ff.

[33] That the external trade—the Silk Trade and the Roman trade—played a significant role in northern India is also clear from the negative evidence. Areas where trade declined as in the Gaṅgā valley shows a decline in the urban economy which has been pointed out by R.S. Sharma. Areas on the northern borders of the sub-continent, arterial to the Central Asian trade flourished in the post-Gupta period.

[34] A comparative regional analysis has become necessary with the recognition not only of regional environmental differences but also variations in the processes of change and the nature of change, particularly the fact that

data has surfaced. What is now required is a sifting and classifying of the data to provide more precise answers and to evoke fresh questions.[35]

---

not all changes coincide chronologically and completely in form. This makes the study of regional history significant not only in terms of regional variations but also as a prerequisite to broader generalizations about the history of the sub-continent.

[35] This work ties in with the debate on feudalism in India, and studies of this period such as those of D.D. Kosambi, R.S. Sharma, B.N.S. Yadava, B.D. Chattopadhyaya, D.N. Jha and H. Mukhia, in addition to many detailed regional studies of the post-Gupta period, too numerous to list here.

Much of the argument on the debate on feudalism in India so far has been of a generalized form. Perhaps what is required at this stage is comparative regional views which could better cope with the areas of investigation which call for analysis. Initially a few selected regions could be analysed in depth for both the urban and the agrarian aspects of the economy, but a start could be made with the agrarian. A tabulation of the data might sharpen the focus. Grants in a region could be classified in accordance with the type of grantee and the nature of the grant. Categories could be defined such as grants of waste land or cultivated land, grants converting lineage-based societies into peasant economies where the grant would be made to the lineage chief, or grants of state-owned lands already cultivated where cultivators were transferred along with the land, and other such categories where data is available. The chronological order and quantum of each would be useful information. Proprietory rights could also be part of this tabulation. At another level the analyses of the titles of grantees and changes therein might provide clues. The question of whether the peasantry was free hinges not only on the technical and legal definitions but also requires a discussion of the actual status of the peasant. Rights, obligations and dues of the grantees vis-à-vis the peasants would need to be tabulated in detail. These would provide some indications of the essentials of the prevailing system.

A worms's eye view of agriculture also needs to be investigated since some aspects of the debate involve questions relating to soil fertility and control over water resources. Some of these questions could be better handled through inter-disciplinary research if historians were to work jointly with specialists in soil analysis, and hydrology. The expertise of a wide range of agricultural scientists has entered into debates on the archaeological evidence relating to agriculture, but curiously has not been invited by agrarian historians into their domain. Now that the study of these subjects has become

It is curious that there is little resort to the policy recommended by the *Arthaśāstra* and other texts of establishing colonies of cultivators on land owned by the state so as to extend agriculture and thereby increase the revenue.[36] Was the state unable to do so because it lacked the administrative infrastructure or was it because it did not have the power to implement such a policy? Instead the state increases the grants of land to religious beneficiaries and later to administrative officers in lieu of a salary. This points to a need for an evaluation of the nature of 'early medieval' states with the possibility that their formation and structure were different from the previous ones. Was this type of state attempting to restructure the economy to an extent greater than the previous which appear to have been more concerned with revenue collecting functions, judging by the model advocated by Kauṭilya? Did the system of granting land predominate (perhaps initially) in

---

so specialized this reluctance as well as the absence of field studies is to be regretted. Considering that the data from survivals of various forms would be much richer for medieval history than for the ancient period one only hopes that a trend in this direction will develop soon. An increase in data of the technical kind can assist the quality of theoretical analysis. Questions more specific to the history of agriculture relate to investigating cultivation techniques, crop patterns, crop rotation, irrigation systems and water cesses, the percentage of arable land available in an area which would condition decisions about starting new settlements or intensifying existing agriculture, variations in the system of fallow for particular crops, the size of holdings in relation to the quality of the soil and the crops, the subsistence level of the peasant, labour input into land and crops and other similar questions. Many of these questions would involve extrapolating back from revenue records as well as considerable field work in the area under study, in order to sharpen the questions and gain insights into possibilities for an earlier period. It is not for nothing that R.H. Tawney is believed to have said that the first essential of research into agrarian history is a pair of stout boots.

[36] Some grants are given of waste land and this would be a case of extending the area under cultivation, but the revenue from this goes to the grantee and not to the state, which makes it different from the situation described in the *Arthaśāstra*. *Śūdra* cultivators are mentioned but in some cases as labourers of land-owners, e.g. Manu IV. 253.

areas where lineage based societies were prevalent so as to facilitate their conversion to a peasant economy (where lineage could also be used for economic control) and to a *varṇa* and *jāti* network? The identification with *varṇa* status would have acted as a bridge to a peasant economy and prevented a rupture with the lineage system. Elements of lineage have often continued even in some areas where peasant agriculture became the norm.

Religious benefices were on the pattern of earlier grants and were not strictly an innovation except that now grants were made increasingly to *brāhmaṇas* and ostensibly in return for legitimizing the dynasty and for acquiring religious merit.[37] These were the stated reasons for the grant but were not sufficient reasons. Grants of this nature, as has been pointed out, were a channel of acculturation. They could also be used as foci of political loyalty.

If the grants were made initially from state-owned lands they amounted to a renouncing of revenue. If the state was unable to administer the extension of agriculture, was the system of grants also introduced to encourage settlements in new areas where the grant was of waste land, or alternatively, of cultivated lands to stabilize the peasantry and induce increased production? Given the fact that slaves were not used in any major quantitative degree in agricultural production at this time, was the system of grants an attempt at converting the peasantry into a stable productive force through various mechanisms of subordination and a chain of intermediaries? Interestingly the term *gahapati*/*gṛhapati* drops out of currency for the system had changed and terms incorporating *rājā, sāmanta* and *bhogin* become frequent. The recipients of land grants had the right to receive a range of taxes and dues previously collected by the state and were soon given administrative powers as well. This permitted them to act as a 'back-up' administration where the grant was in settled areas and to introduce the system

[37] Legitimacy was necessary where the dynasty was of obscure origin or was described as having served the previous one e.g., F.E. Pargiter, *The Purana Texts of the Dynasties of the Kali Age*, Oxford, 1913, pp. 38, 45, 47, 55, 56.

where new settlements were being established. It may in origin have been a fiscal measure but in effect became the means of controlling the peasantry. The apparent increase in debt bondage and the fear of peasant migration would point to this being one of the functions of the large-scale grants. That the possibility of peasant migration to alleviate discontent was being slowly stifled is suggested by the fact of peasants taking to revolt as well from the early second millennium onwards.[38] A rise in brigandage may well have been a possibility for this period.[39] A qualitative change occurs when the state begins to grant villages or substantial acreages of land already under cultivation; a change which reflects both on the economy and on the nature of the state.

The need to fetter the peasantry would seem an evident departure from the earlier system and this in turn introduced a change in the relationship between the cultivator and the land now riveted in legalities and liabilities, with tax or rent no longer being the sole criterion of a peasant economy. The *karṣaka* of this period found himself in a different situation from the *kassaka* of earlier times. The term 'peasant' therefore cannot have a blanket usage or meaning since the variations within it have to be distinguished.

The secular grantees were part of a hierarchical system in which they mirrored the court at the local level. This is evident from their attempts to imitate the courtly style as depicted in the art and literature of the time. Grants of land to the *brāhmaṇa*s as

[38] Instances of such revolts are mentioned in R.S. Sharma, *Indian Feudalism* (Delhi, 1980), pp. 127, 220; cf. N. Karashima, *South Indian History and Society* (New Delhi, 1984). Prior to this the more common form of protest was peasant migration which is referred to in the *Jātaka* literature and which is held out as a threat to a king who demands excessive taxes. Romila Thapar, 'Dissent and Protest in the Early Indian Tradition,' *Studies in History*, 1979, I. No. 2, p. 189ff.

[39] The increasing frequency in hero-stones commemorating a heroic act in defence of a village would point to uncertain conditions in certain areas. These tend to be in the interstices between kingdoms and between settled and forested areas. Romila Thapar, 'Death and the Hero,' in S.C. Humphreys and H. King, eds., *Mortality and Immortality* (London, 1981).

the major religious grantees rehabilitated them to a position of authority and their anguished invocation of Kalki as a millennial figure becomes less urgent.[40] A new religious ideology gained popularity focusing on the image and the temple and asserting an assimilative quality involving the cults and rituals of Purāṇic Hinduism and the genesis of the *bhakti* tradition. Ideological assimilation is called for when there is a need to knit together socially diverse groups. It is also crucial when there is an increase in the distancing between such groups as well as the power of some over others and the economic disparity between them. The significance of these new cults and sects may lie in part in the focus on loyalty to a deity which has a parallel to the loyalty of peasants and others to an overlord. But it would be worth examining the rudiments of each sect in its regional dimension, its grouping towards a *jāti* status and the use of an ostensibly cultural and religious idiom to express a new social identity. Were these also mechanisms for legitimizing territorial identities drawing on sacred geography and pilgrimage routes with the temple as the focal point?[41] The egalitarian emphases of the devotees in the eyes of the deity has rightly been viewed as the assertion of those lower down the social scale in favour of a more egalitarian society. But its significance grows when the social background to this belief is one of increasing disparity. Movements of dissent which had religious forms were often gradually accommodated and their radical content slowly diluted. The move away from community participation in a ritual to a personalized and private worship encourages the notion of individual freedom, even if it is only at the ideological level.

In the justifiable emphasis on social and economic history there has been too frequently a neglect among historians of the

[40] *Viṣṇu Purāṇa* IV. 24; *Mahābhārata*, Śānti Parvan, 254.39ff.

[41] This appears to have become important in a later period judging from the Jagannātha cult at Puri and the Viṭhobā cult at Pandarpur. H. Kulke, *Jagannātha-kult and Gajapati Königtum* (Weisbaden, 1979); G.A. Deleury, *The Cult of Viṭhobā* (Poona, 1960).

analysis of ideology. To study ideology without its historical context is to practice historical hydroponics, for ideas and beliefs strike roots in the humus of historical reality. To restrict the study of a society to its narrowly social and economic forms alone is to see it in a limited two-dimensional profile. The interaction of society and ideology takes a varied pattern and to insist always on the primacy of the one over the other is to deny the richness of a full-bodied historical explanation.

Ideas are sometimes analysed as a response to social pressures and needs. This is particularly pertinent for those dealing with social history. Some of the more important literature is suffused with a theoretical representation of society even in symbolic or ideational forms. Meanings very often do not stem from just the vocabulary but require familiarity with the cultural context of the word. Examples of this would be the levels of meaning of words such as *varṇa* and *jāti* as they travel through time in texts such as the *Dharmaśāstras*. The ideological layers in the latter as codes of behaviour have to be peeled in order to obtain a better comprehension of their ordering of society.

Central to any concern with ideology in the ancient past is the critique of religious thought (as distinct from religious practice or organization). Some analyses of the *Upaniṣads* for instance, can provide an interesting example of this. One of the major strands in Upaniṣadic thought is said to be a secret doctrine known only to a few *kṣatriyas* who teach it to select, trusted *brāhmaṇas*.[42] Even the most learned among the latter, the *mahāśālā mahāśrotriya*, are described as going to the *kṣatriyas* for instruction.[43] The doctrine involves the idea of the soul, the *ātman* and its ultimate merging with the *brahman* as well as metempsychosis or the transmigration of the soul: in fact a fundamental doctrine of this age which was to have far-reaching consequences on Indian society. That it should have been secret and originally associated with the *kṣatriyas* raises

[42] S. Radhakrishnan, *The Principal Upaniṣads* (London, 1953). Introduction.
[43] *Chāndogya Upaniṣad*, V. 11.1ff.

many questions, some of which have been discussed by scholars.[44] It is true that the *brāhmaṇa*s and the *kṣatriya*s were both members of the 'leisured classes' in Vedic society and could therefore indulge in idealistic philosophy and discourse on the niceties of life after death. But this is only a partial answer and much more remains to be explained. Was the ritual of sacrifice so deeply imprinted on the *brāhmaṇa* mind and so necessary to the profession at this point that it required non-*brāhmaṇa*s to introduce alternatives to salvation, other than the sacrificial ritual? The adoption of meditation and theories of transmigration had the advantage of releasing the *kṣatriya*s from the pressures of a prestation economy and permitting them to accumulate wealth, power and leisure. Alternatively, was the accumulation of these already present in the fringe areas, described as the *mlecha-deśa* (impure lands) in Vedic texts, where the sacrificial rituals for various reasons had become less important? Thus Janaka of Mithilā, Aśvapati Kaikeya and Ajātaśatru of Kāśī could reflect on alternative ways to salvation. This also places a different emphasis on the function of the *kṣatriya* who had now ceased to be primarily a cattle-raiding, warrior chief.

These are not the only kinds of connections relevant to a history of the period. Upper and lower groups or even classes treated as monolithic, belie social reality. The tensions within these should also be noticed where the evidence suggests this. The competition for status between *brāhmaṇa*s and *kṣatriya*s and the separation of their functions, as well as their mutual dependence, is symbolized in the sacrificial ritual which becomes a key articulation of the relationship. The new belief was the reversal of the sacrificial ritual in that it required neither priests nor deities but only self-discipline and meditation. At another level, the transmigrating of the soul through the natural elements and plants to

[44] P. Deussen, *The Philosophy of the Upanisads* (Edinburgh, 1906), p. 17ff; A.B. Keith, *Religion and Philosophy of the Vedas* (HOS, 1925), p. 495ff; D.P. Chattopadhyaya, *Indian Philosophy* (New Delhi, 1964), p. 85ff.

its ultimate rebirth, carries an echo of shamanism which may have remained popular outside priestly ritual.

There is in the new belief the first element of a shift from the clan to the individual in as much as the sacrificial ritual involves the clan but meditation and self-discipline, perhaps in opposition to the clan, involves only the individual. It symbolizes the breaking away of the individual from the clan. It also introduces an element of anomie which becomes more apparent in the later development of these beliefs by various sects. These reflections were seminal to what became a major direction in Indian thought and action, the opting out of the individual from society and where renunciation is a method of self-discovery but can also carry a message of dissent.[45] That the new ideas were attributed to the *kṣatriya*s and yet included in a brahmanical text was probably because for the *brāhmaṇa*s to author a doctrine openly questioning the sacrificial ritual would, at this stage, have been an anomaly. That the doctrine stimulated philosophical discussion would in itself have required that it be recorded. But its inclusion may also partially have been motivated by the fact that when the doctrine was appropriated by heterodox teachers such as the Buddha, it could be maintained that even the roots of heterodoxy stemmed from the Vedic tradition. This was to become yet another technique by which orthodox theory in subsequent centuries sought to disguise ideas contradicting its own position. The Buddha not only democratized the doctrine[46] but also nurtured the idea of *karma* and *saṃsāra* and related it, among other things, to social inequities. But his negation of the soul (*ātman*) introduces a contradiction of the doctrine as visualized in the *Upaniṣad*s. Such theoretical contradictions were current at this time.[47] The positing of a thesis and an anti-thesis becomes a characteristic feature of

[45] Romila Thapar, 'Renunciation: the making of a Counter-Culture?' *Ancient Indian Social History: Some Interpretations*, p. 63ff.

[46] S. Radhakrishnan, *op. cit.*

[47] K.N. Jayatilleke, *The Buddhist Theory of Knowledge* (London, 1963), p. 49ff.

philosophical debate and is reflected both in empirical disciplines such as grammar as well as in more abstract analysis.[48]

The relating of ideology to historical reality can result not only in new ways of examining a historical situation and be used to extend or modify the analysis from other sources but can also help in confirming the reality as derived from other sources. (It might also stir the still waters of contemporary interpretations of early Indian thought). Such a study, incorporating elements of deconstructing thought, would sharpen the awareness of concepts and theoretical frameworks. Historical explanation then becomes an enterprise in which the refinements of concepts and theories are a constant necessity, not only because of the availability of fresh evidence from new sources but also because of greater precision in our understanding of the categories which we use to analyse these sources. It is a bi-focal situation where the frame of reference provided by the analysis of ideology remains the distant view while the historian's use of a theoretical explanation of the data indicates the nearer reading.

[48] S.D. Joshi (ed.) *Patañjali's Vyākaraṇa Mahābhaṣya* (Poona, 1968), pp. i–xiv. At the more abstract level it is evident in the Brahmajālasutta in the *Dīgha Nikāya* I.1. The method of *pūrvapakṣa-uttarapakṣa-siddhānta,* although reminiscent of Hegel's dialectic should not be taken as an equivalent as it appears to have been limited to categories of logical analysis.

*Society and Historical Consciousness: The Itihāsa-purāṇa Tradition**

The expression of historical consciousness, it has often been assumed, takes the form of historical writing, clearly recognizable as a genre of literature. More frequently, however, the geological analogy of a particular vein embedded in rock seems more apposite, in that such consciousness is not always visible and has to be prised from sources which tend to conceal it. Within the vein lies information purporting to relate to events of the past, and enveloping this vein is the commentary which arises from concerns of the present. The form it takes tends to reflect the kind of society from which it emanates.

Historical consciousness, therefore, can change over time. Historians tend to view historical writing as conforming almost entirely to the format and pattern familiar from the last couple of centuries, or from models borrowed from particular societies such as ancient Greece and China. The more important but neglected aspect is the search for historical consciousness, irrespective of how immediately recognizable or evident it may be, in its literary form. This perhaps requires a distinction between what might be termed 'embedded history'—forms in which historical conscious-

* I am grateful to my colleagues Satish Saberwal and B.D. Chattopadhyaya for comments on an earlier draft of this essay.

ness has to be prised out—and its opposite, 'externalized history'—which tends to bring embedded consciousness into the open, as it were, and to be more aware of its deliberate use of the past. The need for such a deliberate use suggests a changed historical situation. This distinction can be apparent not only between societies but also within the same society as it undergoes change. The attempt in this essay is not to analyse historical consciousness in relation to society as a whole, but in relation to a more restricted view of its expression among those who successfully aspired to power. It relates therefore only to historical writing in terms of changing forms in the perception of power.

Each version of the past which has been deliberately transmitted has a significance for the present, and this accounts for its legitimacy and its continuity. The record may be one in which historical consciousness is embedded: as in myth, epic and genealogy; or alternatively it may refer to the more externalized forms: chronicles of families, institutions and regions, and biographies of persons in authority. There is no evolutionary or determined continuum from one form to the other and facets of the embedded consciousness can be seen as a part of the latter, whether introduced deliberately or subconsciously. The degree to which forms change or overlap has a bearing on dominant social formations. Similarly, major social and political changes influence the form of historical consciousness even though there is no mechanical correlation between the two.

Evident historical texts such as chronicles of families, institutions and regions often incorporate mythical beginnings which act as charters of validation. The tracing of links with established lineages through genealogical connections, and frequently with epic heroes, plays the same role of drawing upon embedded history. I shall consider some forms of embedded history, such as the prevalent myths in the *itihāsa-purāṇa* tradition, which encapsulate features of what might be seen as historical experience; the eulogies and hero-lauds which were gradually expanded into epic literature; the genealogical sections or *vaṁśānucarita* of the Puranic texts which, by implication, carry a commentary on the social status of ruling families.

In contrast to these the more externalized forms draw upon the embedded but have other primary concerns and carry a different type of historical information. Thus historical biography or the *carita* literature has as its germ the hero-laud and the epic hero. Family chronicles and *vaṃśāvalīs* assimilate myth and genealogy to other events. Chronicles of institutions and regions maintain a variant form of mythology and genealogy, and are aimed at recording the history of the institution or the area. The distinction made between the two forms is not arbitrary; I am arguing that the embedded form is closer to what have been called lineage-based societies and the externalized form to state systems incorporated in monarchies. Or, to put it in another way, the existence of the state requiring its own validation encourages the creation of an externalized historical consciousness.

In the articulation of historical consciousness in early north-Indian society the truly embedded forms are evident in the literature of the lineage-based society characterized by an absence of state formation, and the more free-standing or externalized forms emerge with the transition to state systems. The terms 'lineage society' and 'state systems', used here as a short-hand, represent not merely a change in political forms but a multiple social change. Thus the term 'state' would refer to a society registering political polarities, an increasingly vertical hierarchy of authority, social inequalities, differentiated economies and distinct ideological identities; not that these characteristics are completely absent in lineage societies, but there are endemic differences between the two. Sometimes these differences are blurred in the texts. Lineage society derives its validity from different sources of authority as compared to state systems, with which we are in any case more familiar.[1] The central role of lineage in the earlier society has

[1] I have discussed these differences as they pertain to early Indian society, specifically to Vedic and post-Vedic times prior to the rise of the Mauryan state, in *From Lineage to State* (Delhi, 1984). The term 'lineage' is used in

reference to more than just the ordering of kinship for it dominates virtually every aspect of activity.

I

The deepest layer of the embedded form is myth. Events are assumed to have happened, and time is almost proto-chronos since it involves gods and the supernatural in an active role with humans and animals. The significance of myth to the historian lies more in its being the self-image of a given culture, expressing its social assumptions. The role of myth in this context is often explanatory. Origin myths are concerned with cosmogony and the start of events such as the Flood myth.[2] The *Śatapatha Brāhmaṇa* version of the Flood myth carries obvious traces of association with the Sumerian Flood myth. Manu, when performing his morning ablutions, finds a fish in his cupped hands and rears the fish until it reaches an enormous size. The fish explains the intention of the gods to drown the earth in a deluge and, wishing to save Manu and the seven *ṛṣis* (in whom vests all knowledge) from this disaster, it orders Manu to build a boat for this purpose. This is tied to its horn and it swims through the deluge. The boat and its passengers remain safely on a mountain until the flood subsides, after which they return. By means of sacrifical rites Manu creates a series of sons for himself and one androgynous daughter, his children being the founders of the various lineages. The eldest son, Ikṣvāku, establishes the Sūryavaṃśa or Solar lineage, and the androgynous daughter, Ilā/Iḍa, establishes the Candravaṃśa or Lunar lineage.

preference to the more commonly employed term 'tribe', as lineage whether fictive or real is central to such societies, is more precise and points to the crux of such societies where descent and birth are in fact the major focus of social ordering.

2 '*Śatapatha Brāhmaṇa* I.8.1.1–10; *Mahābhārata*, Sabhāparvan, 185; *Matsya Purāṇa* I.11–34; Romila Thapar, 'Puranic Lineages and Archaeological Cultures,' in *Ancient Indian Social History: Some Interpretations* (New Delhi 1978) (hereafter referred to as *AISH*), p. 240 ff.

The *Matsya Purāṇa* version links the fish with the incarnation of Viṣṇu, thus bringing the gods more directly into the story, and at the same time using what was obviously a familiar myth to demonstrate the power of the new god, Viṣṇu. Manu, as the name suggests in its association with *mānava* (mankind), is the primeval, archetypal man who is the eponymous ancestor of all the lineages. The emphasis on origins is again stressed in the deluge, where the flood is seen as a time-marker. Floods tend to wipe away earlier conditions and society can start afresh.[3] The survival of Manu and the *ṛṣi*s links the new creation with the old, in spite of the deluge washing away the old, since Manu is the seventh in a succession of pre-Flood Manus. The link is important to the genealogical records. The status of the earlier Manus is conveyed through it to the new lineages. All the eponymous ancestors of the lineages are the children of Manu.

Other myths provide social sanctions, one such being the Puruṣasūkta story in the *Ṛg Veda* describing the origin of the four castes.[4] The Puruṣasūkta hymn occurs in a late section of the *Ṛg Veda* and describes the sacrifice of the god Prajāpati, from whose body the four *varṇa*s are said to have sprung: the *brāhmaṇa*s from his mouth, the *kṣatriya*s from his arms, the *vaiśya*s from his thighs and the *śūdra*s from his feet. The symbolism of each bodily part relates to the ritual status and function of the particular *varṇa*. That the origin and hierarchy go back to a ritual occasion underlines the nature of the ranking. The evolution of *varṇa* stratification is rooted in the lineage-based society of Vedic times. In a sense the *brāhmaṇa* and the *kṣatriya varṇa*s were to evolve as distinct lineages with their separate rules of marriage and descent: exogamy in the *brāhmaṇa gotra*s and the more frequent endogamy of the *kṣatriya*s. The *śūdra varṇa* is excluded by its very origin, which is a denial of lineage since it is said more often to include groups identified by the status of the two parents.

[3] M. Eliade, *The Myth of the Eternal Return* (Princeton, 1971).
[4] *Ṛg Veda*, x. 97.

Some myths legitimize a changed social and political condition, as is apparent from the much repeated story of Pṛthu.[5] The various versions of this story begin by referring to the wickedness of Vena who had to be killed by the *ṛṣis* because of his unrighteous rule. From his left thigh they churned a successor, Niṣāda, who was inadequate and was expelled to the forest as a hunter-gatherer. From the right arm of Vena they churned another successor, the righteous *rājā* Pṛthu, who introduced cattle-keeping and agriculture and bestowed so many benefits on the earth, Pṛthvī, that she in gratitude gave him her name. Vena was wicked because he ceased to perform the sacrificial ritual and had to be killed by the *ṛṣis* (and not expelled by his subjects), who alone had the right to depose a ruler. The dark, short, ugly Niṣāda became the prototype of all forest-dwelling people. The myth sought to legitimize the expulsion of such groups when land was cleared and settled by agriculturists.

In each of such cases an attempt is made to explain social origins and assumptions which are significant to historical reconstruction. Myth was transmitted orally in its earliest phase. With the evolution of a more heterogeneous and stratified society, myths were questioned and explanations sought. Some myths were replaced with new or different versions and others added to and embellished, often to such a degree that the original myth became almost opaque. That myths in some ways mirrored society was not their sole function, but for our purposes this aspect is significant.

Myths of descent often serve to integrate diverse groups by providing common origins. Among competing groups a myth can be used for the reverse process of distinguishing one from the other. Origin myths posit beginnings authoritatively and are therefore central to embedded history. The degree to which myths reflect different social assumptions can be demonstrated by a comparison of origin myths from the *Ṛg Veda* and from Buddhist

[5] *Mahābhārata*, Śāntiparvan, 59: *Viṣṇu Purāṇa*, I.13; *Matsya Purāṇa*, x.4–10.

sources, a comparison which also demonstrates the degree to which historical consciousness is embedded in myth.[6] The origins of the Śākyas, Licchavis, Mallas and Koliyas are all described in stories which have a common format, which format suggests a tradition deviant from the brahmanical origin myths. The clans are of the Ikṣvāku lineage, are said to be of the families of *rājā*s (which could mean royal descent but more likely refers to families of lineage chiefs) and are often the exiled children of such families, thus suggesting a lineage migration or fission. The new settlement is in a forest clearing with a town as its nucleus. The name of the lineage is frequently associated with an object such as the *kol* or *śaka* tree. More interestingly, the original founders have a system of sibling marriages and in each case sixteen pairs of twin children are born: it is from these that the lineage expands. Sibling incest, since it is never actually referred to as prevalent, would point to a symbolic concern with purity of lineage, a demarcation between the families of the *rājā*s who owned land and the rest of the people, by the assertion of origins otherwise taboo; or perhaps an endorsement of cross-cousin marriage, which, because it was prohibited by brahmanical codes referring to northern India, may have been seen as a form of sibling incest. That the origin myth was of some consequence is evident from its inclusion in the history of every lineage and by the considerable emphasis given to it in the biographies of the Buddha. There is an absence of any reference to ritual status.

II

Apart from myth, other embedded forms are associated with various fragments of literature moving towards the emergence of the epic. The evolution is traceable via the *dāna-stuti* (eulogies on

[6] *Sutta Nipāta*, 420ff; *Sutta Nipāta Commentary*, I.352ff; *Sumaṅgalavilāsinī*, I, pp. 258–60; Romila Thapar, 'Origin Myths and the Historical Tradition,' *AISH*, p. 294ff.

gift-giving), *gāthā*, *nārāśaṁsi* (eulogies on heroes) to the *ākhyāna* and the *kathā* (cycles of stories generally involving heroes). The *dāna-stuti* hymns scattered throughout the *Ṛg Veda* are eulogies on chiefs and deities who act as would chiefs bestowing generous gifts on grateful bards and priests.[7] The prototype of the gift-giver was the god Indra. The Indra-*gāthā*s express the gratitude of the *jana* (tribe) whom he has led successfully in a cattle-raid and subsequently in distributing the wealth bestowed, much of it on the priests. The same was expected from the ideal *rājā* (chief) in a society where raids were a major access to property and where wealth was computed in heads of cattle and horse, in chariots, gold and slave girls. The *dāna-stuti*s mentioned the names of their patrons, who were doubtless actual chiefs, but, equally important, the hymns indicated the purpose of the gift and the items of wealth. They were not only eulogies of past actions but also indicators of what was expected from the chiefs.

The *ākhyāna*s, commemorating *rājā*s and heroes, were the cycles of stories recited at the time of the *yajña*s (sacrificial rituals).[8] Some heroes underwent a metamorphosis in time and came to be remembered for reasons quite different from those of the earliest stories. Thus Purūravas in the *Ṛg Veda* is a mortal who loves a celestial woman, Urvaśi; in the *Śatapatha Brāhmaṇa* he is shown as aspiring to become a celestial being himself in pursuit of his love; and finally in the *Mahābhārata* he is not only a celestial being but is among the more important ancestors of the Candravaṁśa lineage.[9] The protagonists in these stories are members of the chiefly families (*rājanya*s and *kṣatriya*s); the stories narrate their lives and activities and incidentally provide information on the lineages as

[7] *Ṛg Veda*, VI. 63; V. 27; V. 30; VI. 47; VIII. 1; VIII. 5; VIII.6.

[8] Both the terms *ākhyāna* and *kathā* have the meaning of recitation or oral narration, and the purpose of the form is clear from these words. Some of the bardic fragments in the form of stories are also to be found in the *Jātaka* literature.

[9] *Ṛg Veda*, X. 95; *Śatapatha Brāhmaṇa*, XI. 5.1.1ff; *Mahābhārata*, Ādiparvan, VII. 70–71.

well. An example of the latter is the transformation of single lineages into confederacies of tribes—the Bharatas and the Pūrus of the *Ṛg Veda* confederating with others into the Kurus of later times. The genealogies tend to be shallow and activities centre around the lineages rather than the succession of hereditary status.

A common feature of these many embedded forms is that they are linked to the ritual of sacrifice, the *yajña*. This imparts sanctity to the story and ensures it a continuity coeval with the performance of the ritual; it also imbues it with what were believed to be transcendental powers associated with the accurate and precise performance of the ritual. Even if the events were limited to the activities of the *kṣatriya*s, the audience was much wider and incorporated the entire tribe. Apart from the obvious ritual and religious function of the *yajña* its relevance also lay in its being the occasion for the redistribution of wealth, both from cattle raids and from agricultural production. Up to a point certain rituals had elements of a potlatch in which wealth was not merely redistributed but was also consumed. Both the redistribution as well as the destruction of wealth were directly concerned with claims to status.[10]. When the ritual was enlarged to include representation from other *jana*s, either in the form of honoured guests or as tribute bearers, its function as a potlatch gradually gave way to its symbolizing status on a grander scale. The claims ot individual lineages or their segments as descent groups could be established on such occasions, as for example the famous *rājasūya* sacrifice of Yudhiṣṭhira[11] which raises a complex set of problems concerning the status of various lineages, not least among them that of Kṛṣṇa as the chief of the Vṛṣṇis. The *yajña* therefore stated, as it were, the ranking order of the lineages. The stories which related to these lineages became social charters recording status *vis-à-vis* other lineages, or changes of status, as for example from segment to confederacy, or the migration and fissioning off of a segment from

[10] Romila Thapar, '*Dāna* and *dakṣiṇa* as forms of exchange,' in *AISH*, p. 105ff.

[11] *Mahābhārata*, Sabhāparvan, 30ff; 34ff.

a lineage, as in the case of the Cedis migrating from the western Ganga valley to central India.[12] The record of such migrations was crucial not only to territorial claims but also to genealogical links with established lineages by those newly formed. The *yajña* was a conduit of gift-exchange as well where the wealth of the lineage brought as *bali* or tribute (initially voluntary and later less so) by the *viś* (clan) to the *kṣatriya* or the *rājā*, or else the wealth captured in a raid would be ceremonially used in the ritual and what remained of it would be gifted to the *brāhmaṇas* performing the *yajña*. The exchange was at many levels. Wealth was offered to the gods in return for the success and well-being both of the *kṣatriya* and the *viś*, the well being guaranteed by the *brāhmaṇas*. Tangible wealth moved from the household of the *kṣatriya* to that of the *brāhmaṇa*. Such a limited exchange was economically non-productive in the sense that it was self-perpetuating with little chance of breaking through to new social forms. But its actual significance lay in its being an operative process in maintaining the lineage society.

III

It was doubtless these fragments of eulogies (*praśastis*) on the heroes and the cycles of stories which led to the first gropings towards epic forms in India, referred to as the *kathā*. Both the *Mahābhārata* and the *Rāmāyaṇa* had their earlier and perhaps more truly epic versions in what have been referred to as the *Rāma-kathā* and the *Bhārata*[13] or *Jaya*. In their later forms, as we have them

[12] *Mahābhārata*, Ādiparvan, 57.

[13] V.S. Sukthankar, *On the Meaning of the Mahabharata* (Bombay, 1957); 'Epic Studies,' *ABORI*, XVIII, pp. 1–76; C. Bulke, *Rāma-kathā* (Allahabad, 1972); H. Jacobi, *The Ramayana* (trans. S.N. Ghoshal), (Baroda, 1960). It is a moot question as to how much of the original epic persists in the now heavily inflated and interpolated versions, which, despite the critical editions of both texts, still require substantial pruning to be brought anywhere near the original. The interpolations have been both of substance and form: hence the

now, each of the two epics has a distinct locale and the narrative is woven around one of the two main lineages. Thus the *Mahābhārata* focuses on the western Gaṅgā valley, referred to as *madhya-deśa* in the literature, and is concerned with the Aila lineage. The *Rāmāyaṇa* as the epic of the Ikṣvāku lineage has its nucleus in the middle Gaṅgā valley, in Kośala and Videha, and is concerned with migrations southwards into the Vindhyan region, with Dakṣina Kośala perhaps providing the clue to the area of exile.

The epic continued to be recited, initially on ritual occasions; the *Mahābhārata* is said to have been recited at the *yajña* in the Naimiśa forest and the *sarpa-yajña* of Janamejaya, the *Rāmāyaṇa* by Lava and Kuśa in the Vālmīki-*āśrama*. But it also became the stock for court poetry, the *kāvya,* in the newly emerging courts of the monarchies of the late first millennium BC, or for that matter in more elaborate literary fashions in the courts of the various kingdoms of the first millennium AD.

The epic form carries within it the germs of a more conscious and less embedded historical tradition.[14] Its historicity lies in the fact that it is a later age reflecting on an earlier one, the reflections frequently taking the form of interpolations interleaved among the

---

reference to the *Rāmāyaṇa* as a *kāvya* or literary poem and to the *Mahābhārata* as *itihāsa*, more closely approximating history, although the historical content remains internalized.

[14] This is in part reflected in the perennial search by archeologists for 'epic ages'. The financially flourishing 'Ramayana archaeology', even though without any tangible results, continues to be discussed seriously in some archaeological and historical circles, despite the near absurdity of the idea. That epic archaeology is an almost non-existent category becomes clear from a discussion of the encrustations which go into the making of an epic. E.W. Hopkins, *The Great Epic of India: Its Character and Origin* (New York, 1901); V.S. Sukthankar, *Prolegomena* to the Critical Edition of Adi Parvan (Poona, 1933); Romila Thapar, *Exile and the Kingdom: Some Thoughts on the Rāmāyaṇa* (Bangalore, 1978); 'The Historian and the Epic,' *Annals of the Bhandarkar Oriental Research Institute*, 1979, vol. LX, pp. 199–213; B.D. Chattopadhyaya, 'Indian Archaeology and the Epic Tradition,' *Puratattva*, VIII, 1975–6, pp. 67–71.

fragments of the oral, bardic tradition. When epic literature ceases to be a part of the oral tradition and is frozen into a written form, reflections begin to tail off. The pastoral-agricultural society of the world of the heroes structured around lineage gives way to the more clearly agrarian societies and to the rise of urban centres controlled by what is visibly emerging as a state system—which in the Gaṅgā valley at this time was mainly monarchical.

Many of the seeming contradictions in the stances and configurations characterizing the epics can perhaps be explained by these texts (and particularly the *Mahābhārata*), reflecting something of a transitional condition between two rather different structures, the societies of the lineage-based system and that of the monarchical state. Idealized characters are seldom the gods but rather the heroes who occupy the centre of the stage and the gods remain in the wings. Sometimes the earlier deities even come in for a drubbing.[15] The importance of the heroes is further endorsed by their being almost the terminal descendants in the major lineages of the past, a matter of some despair for their death is seen as the wrapping up and putting away of the lineage society, which, in certain areas, was being replaced by monarchies. However, some elements of the lineage society did persist and among them was the continuation of *varṇa* ranking. In many areas outside the *madhya-deśa*, lineage society continued for longer periods and the transition to monarchical states was a gradual process. Nevertheless the change to monarchy meant a substantial alteration of social configurations.

Unlike myth, epic does not attempt to explain the universe or society. It is sufficient that the problems of society are laid bare, and even solutions are not sought since the ultimate solution is the

[15] The treatment of Indra in the epics, for example, records a sea change from the Indra-*gāthās* of the *Ṛg Veda*. Indra is now subservient not only to the rising status of Viṣṇu but is unequal even to the superior power of the *ṛṣis*. Leaving aside the deliberate incarnating of Viṣṇu as the epic heroes Rāma and Kṛṣṇa, there is little doubt that they are now more central than the older gods.

dissolution of the system. Societies experiencing greater stratification require an overall authority to maintain the cohesion of lineage and strata. When such an authority comes into being and is eulogized, that eulogy becomes the dirge of a truly epic society. In laying bare the conditions in the transition from lineage society to state systems, a number of bi-polarities are reflected in the literature which give an added edge to the image of the past and the contours of the present. Thus *grāma* (settlement) is contrasted with *aranya* (forest), the kingdom with exile; the orderliness of the *grāma* is opposed to the disorder of the *aranya;* the kingly ethic arises out of governing a people and claiming land, the heroic ethic emerges from war and confrontation. The monarchical state is seen as the superior and is the successor to lineage society, irrespective of whether this is clearly spelt out—as in the conflict between the kingdom of Kośala and the *rākṣasas* in the *Rāmāyaṇa*—or whether it is left more ambiguous—as in the diverse assumptions of the narrative and didactic sections of the *Mahābhārata* where the Ṣabhāparvan, encapsulating the essence of a lineage society, stands in contrast to the Śāntiparvan with its rhetoric on the monarchical state. The new ethic is sustained in part by the popularizing of new sources of authority. Among them and significant to the political arena were the king, the *brāhmaṇa* and the *ṛṣi*. None of these were entirely new in that the chief, the priest and the shaman were dominant figures in lineage society. But it is the tangible authority of the king based on land as the source of revenue, or of the *brāhmaṇa* as the sole performer of and manual on rituals, and of the *ṛṣi* and *saṁnyāsi* as symbolizing an intangible moral authority almost as a counterweight to that of the first two, which gives a fresh dimension to their role and their interrelations. The changed situation is reflected in a shift in the kind of authority exercised. From a more diffused, equitable authority there is a movement towards a hierarchical, vertical authority.[16] This was

[16] Cf. W.B. Miller, 'Two Concepts of Authority,' *American Anthropologist*, April 1955, vol. 57, pp. 271–89.

mitigated somewhat by the countervailing presence of the renouncer and the charisma attached to renunciation.

The epic as the literature of one age looking back nostalgically on another can become a literature of legitimation. Interpolations are often the legitimation of the present but are attributed to the heroes of the past. The bards were perhaps providing the models of what patrons should be like. But, more important, it is the kingdoms looking back on an age of chiefships: where recently founded dynasties were seeking ancestry from the *kṣatriya* lineages through actual or, more often, imagined genealogical links; where such ancestry would also bestow social legitimacy and validate kingship. That legitimacy and validation are essential to the epic is clear from the central event of the narrative, namely the legitimacy of succession, involving elder and younger sons and the problems of disqualification.[17] Legitimacy also relates to using the past to explain the present. Perhaps the most dramatic example of this is the series of explanations in favour of accepting the strangeness of Draupadī marrying five brothers, fraternal polyandry not being a commonly practised form of marriage. Among the explanations is predictably a reference to an earlier birth of Draupadī.[18] Fortunately the doctrine of transmigration, referring to events and situations in a previous birth, makes the use of the past more plausible. The interplay of the past and the present is thus not only part of the implicit epic idiom but is made more explicit by recourse to the theory of transmigration. At another

[17] J.A.B. van Buitenan refers to the problem of the 'disqualified eldest' in his introduction to the translation of the Ādiparvan. The *Mahābhārata. The Book of the Beginning* (Chicago, 1973), p. xviii. The problem goes back to earlier antecedents. Thus the Candravaṁśa lineage starts with the replacement of Yadu, the eldest son of Yayāti, by his youngest son, Pūru. The *Mahābhārata* war, which involves virtually all the *kṣatriya* lineages and becomes the last heroic act of a lineage society, is again motivated by the problem of succession where physical ailments further complicate the question. The exile of Rāma is over the issue of succession, which, in spite of the heavier emphasis on primogeniture, is still subject to the whims and wishes of the parents.

[18] *Mahābhārata*, Ādiparvan, 189.

level the past validates the present in the long discourses on what constitutes good government or the correct functioning of the *kṣatriya* as king: perhaps best exemplified in the dying Bhīṣma delivering the lengthy *mokṣadharma* perorations, lying on his bed of arrows. Legitimacy makes the claim to historicity more feasible and the association with myth is weakened.[19]

IV

The gradual prising of historical consciousness becomes visible in the compilation of what came to be called the *itihāsa-purāṇa*.[20] The phrase remains difficult to define, veering between the perceived past and historicity. It is described as the fifth Veda but was an oral tradition for many centuries until it was compiled in the form of the *Purāṇa*s in the mid first millennium AD. The genealogical sections of the *Purāṇa*s were a reordering of the earlier material in a new format. The lesser and multiple *Purāṇa*s borrowed the format of the earlier major *Purāṇa*s, although their contents differed. The *Purāṇa* was to become a recognized literary form. To the extent that it recorded history, it was initially transitional from embedded to externalized history. It was linked to the bardic tradition, where the *sūta* and the *māgadha* are said to have been its earliest authors.[21] In the Vedic texts the *sūta* has a close relation with the *rājā* and was of high status, but by the time of the Manu *Dharmaśāstra* the *sūta* had been reduced to the level of a *sankīrṇa*-

[19] Romila Thapar, 'The *Rāmāyaṇa*: Theme and Variation,' in S.N. Mukherjee, ed., *India: History and Thought* (Calcutta, 1982), pp. 221–53.

[20] The *itihāsa-purāṇa* is referred to in the *Arthaśāstra*, 1.5. Its literal meaning is 'thus it was'—*iti-hi-asa*. The events of the past were to be so related as to link them with the goals and purposes of the tradition which was being historicised.

[21] The *sūta* and the *māgadha* are said to have arisen from the sacrifice of Pṛthu, and immediately on appearing began a *praśasti* of the *rājā*. *Atharvaveda*, V.3.5.7; *Taittirīya Brāhmaṇa*, II.4.1. In texts such as *Gautama*, IV.15; *Manu*, X.11, 26; *Nārada*, 110, the status of the *sūta* has changed. This change is made explicit in the *Mahābhārata*, Ādiparvan, 122.4ff. and 126.15ff., in which the *sūta* is inferior to the *kṣatriya*.

jāti or mixed caste. Doubtless by now the tradition had been appropriated by the literate *brāhmaṇas* who had also seen the potential value of controlling oral information on the past and recording it in a literary form relevant to emergent contemporary requirements.

There is evidence to suggest that the Purāṇic texts were translated from the oral Prākrit to the literate Sanskrit.[22] The structure of the *Purāṇas* was an attempt to provide an integrated world view of the past and present, linking events to the emergence of a deity or a sect, since each *Purāṇa* was dedicated to such a one, the *Viṣṇu Purāṇa* being regarded as the model. The historical epicentre of the *itihāsa* tradition was the *vaṁśānucarita*, which, as the name suggests, was the genealogy of all the known lineages and dynasties upto the mid-first millennium AD. It was not a parallel tradition to the earlier *kathās* and *ākhyānas* since it incorporated many of these forms of embedded history. The genealogical core pertaining to those who were believed to have held power in the past was carefully preserved after it had been worked out into a systematic pattern. This was because it not only purported to record the past but was also later to become essential to future claims to lineage status, and was therefore linked with historical writing. Evidently there was a need for a recognizable historical tradition at this time. In the transition from lineage to state, which was occurring in many parts of north India, monarchy had emerged as the viable political form.

The major dynasties recorded in the *Purāṇas* upto the mid-first millennium AD start with descendants of recognized *kṣatriya* lineages, but by the mid-first millennium BC begin to refer to families of non-*kṣatriya* origin. Some are specifically said to be *śūdras*, such as the Nandas and possibly the Mauryas. Others, judging by their names, were *brāhmana*, such as the Śuṅgas and Kāṇvas. The lesser dynasties dating to the early centuries AD are stated to be *vrātya-dvija*, *śūdra* and *mleccha*, and this is explained as resulting from the

[22] F.E. Pargiter, *The Ancient Indian Historical Tradition* (London, 1922), p. 77ff; *Dynasties of the Kali Age* . . . , 1913, reprint, (Delhi, 1975), p. 77ff.

inevitable degeneration of all norms in the Kaliyuga. Successor dynasties are frequently referred to as the *bhṛtyas* or servants of the previous ones, suggesting that the founders of dynasties may often have been administrators, high in the hierarchy of office who overthrew weak kings. This may well account for the rise of *brāhmaṇa* dynasties. The gradual increase in references to *śūdra* rulers would indicate that political power, although in theory restricted to *kṣatriya*s, was infact open to any *varṇa*. It required force and administrative control to establish a dynasty. Claims to territory were established through strength of arms. Legitimation through brahmanical ritual was evidently not required since some dynasties are described as not conforming to Vedic rites. This may well have been due to the influence of Buddhism and Jainism at this time. The Brahmanical refusal to bestow *kṣatriya* status on such families may have been in part due to their being patrons of non-brahmanical religious sects. Buddhist and Jaina literature on the other hand insists on the *kṣatriya* status of some of these dynasties. Thus the Mauryas are not only listed as *kṣatriya*s but are linked to the clan of the Buddha, the Śākyas, which would automatically have related them to the prestigious Sūryavaṁśa as well.[23] The absence of proper status in the brahmanical sources did not detract from the importance of these families. If anything it points to the relative independence of the state as a political form from the clutches of traditional validation during this period. The need for legitimation through lineage status was apparently not required at this time.

The encroachment of foreign rulers in the post-Mauryan period led to some indigenous families having to recede into the background. Claims to power and to actual status were conceded to the Indo-Greeks, Śakas, Parthians and Kuṣāṇas, but claim to *varṇa* status was denied them and they continued to be called *vrātya-kṣatriya*s (degenerate), having no indigenous land-base in the sub-continent nor being able to claim kinship links with earlier

[23] *Mahāvaṁsaṭīkā*, p. 180ff.

established lineages.[24] This was despite the fact that some among them did claim *kṣatriya* status in their own inscriptions.[25] The lack of genealogical connections was a form of exclusion, effective in a society where ritual status still drew heavily on the values of a lineage-based social organization and where genealogical links had played a crucial role.

Although dynastic status was not confined to any particular *varṇa*, those who succeeded to kingship from the mid-first millennium AD onwards often observed the formality of claiming *kṣatriya* status, or at least of participating in a common *kṣatriya* past as embodied in the *itihāsa-purāṇa* tradition. The question may well be asked as to why such a practice becomes more necessary during this period, and the answer covers a range of possibilities. The making of land grants to *brāhmaṇa*s and the consequent spread of Sanskritic culture provides an obvious reason. But it would be as well not to overlook the reality on the ground, as it were, and examine the actual process of state formation at a time when it related to secondary (if not tertiary) states, or new states emerging from association with established states. Land grants of a substantial size to non-religious grantees would have provided the base for the grantee establishing a network of political control over the area through his lineage connections.[26] The partial *brāhmaṇa* ancestry of some ruling families as given in their genealogies would suggest that even *brāhmaṇa* grantees were not averse to participating in this process. Where unoccupied land was still available and the migration of peasants feared, political control would be less effective if dependent on force and more effective if drawing its strength from legitimacy. The expression of power in the sense of controlling resources and seeking compliance through persuasion, influence and support[27] would be better achieved by

[24] *Viṣṇu Purāṇa*, IV. 21–4: *Manu*, X. 43–5.

[25] *Epigraphia Indica*, VIII, pp. 59, 86; E.J. Rapson, ed., *The Cambridge History of India*, vol. I, *Ancient India* (Cambridge, 1935), p. 577.

[26] For a later period, cf. R.G. Fox, *Kin, Clan, Raja and Rule* (Berkeley, 1971)

[27] Miller, *op cit*.

legitimacy than by force. The legitimation of lineage origins therefore became a necessity.

The granting of land, apart from its other functions, served also to incorporate areas under lineage systems into the society dominated by the state. Lineage-based agrarian activity was assimilated into the new economy and erstwhile clansmen or else their chiefs were converted into tax-paying peasants. Lineage traditions continued up to a point and could be adjusted to the *varṇa* framework, which acted as a bridge between the earlier society and its later form.

It would be worth investigating whether the process of state formation in the late first millennium AD provided a different emphasis from that of the earlier period. The overlap between lineage and state continued, but the political form was perhaps not so reliant on institutions of the state and included a more substantial dependence on lineage. Would it then be correct to argue that the post-Gupta state did not attempt to uproot the *kṣatriyas* (to use the phrase of the *Purāṇas*) and reduce the importance of lineage societies, but rather that it attempted to encourage the emergence of a new role for lineages through which it sought to extend its control?

With the kaleidoscopic formation of states in the post-Gupta period, new ruling families relied heavily on genealogical links, fabricated genealogies providing them with claims to being *kṣatriyas*: claims which were carefully stated in the then legal charters, i.e. the inscriptions recording the grants of land by these families to *brāhmaṇas* and other grantees. Such claims became even more crucial in a situation of competition for status by horizontal marriage alliances among the 'new' *kṣatriyas*. Matrimonial links sealed the claims to status. Thus the possible tribal Gond and Bhil associations of the Candella and Guhilot ruling families did not eventually stand in the way of their claims to *kṣatriya* status, which were backed not merely by land-ownership but also by claims to genealogical links with the Candravaṁśa and the Sūryavaṁśa: the claim being recognized with marriage into other established *kṣatriya* families.[28] The sixteenth century marriage of a Gond *rājā* into the Candella family is an interesting example of how the system worked. The acceptance by other competing families of the origin myth and of the genealogy of the family successfully installed in power was largely because political power was relatively open and individual families were concerned with succeeding to power, not with altering the framework within which status was conferred. The narrowing down of legitimation to one family meant that others could aspire to the same power in changed circumstances.

The earlier states from the Mauryan to the Kuṣāṇa tended to develop administrative structures in which local regions were left relatively untampered as long as they provided the required revenue.[29] When revenue requirements became oppressive, peasants could threaten to migrate from the state and establish new clearings in the forest and on waste land. Migration was the alternative to peasant revolt and kings are cautioned against oppressive taxes lest peasants migrate. From the Gupta period onwards there was a gradual and increasing tendency to intensify the revenue demands and tie down the peasantry.[30] The economic restructuring of the local region was regarded as part of the state's legitimate right to revenue. The ability of the peasant to migrate was hampered, and even though there is little apparent evidence of peasant

[28] J.N. Asopa, *Origin of the Rajputs* (Delhi, 1976) pp. 102ff., 208ff; J. Tod, *Annals and Antiquities of Rajasthan*, vol. I, (London, 1960), p. 173ff. Asopa argues that 'Guhila' means a forest and that it is to be located in the area between Guhila-bala and the Mahi river. See also B.D. Chattopadhyaya, 'Origin of the Rajput: The Political, Economic and Social Processes in Early Medieval Rajasthan,' *The Indian Historical Review*, July, 1976, vol. III, no. 1, pp. 59–82. Claims to *kṣatriya* status were also made by ruling families and politically powerful groups in south India. Thus the Colas claimed to be Sūryavaṁśi, the Pāṇḍyas Candravaṁśi, and the *vel* chieftains sought Yādava descent.

[29] Romila Thapar, 'The State as Empire,' in H. Claessen and P. Skalnik, *The Study of the State* (The Hague, 1981), p. 409ff.

[30] R.S. Sharma, *Indian Feudalism* (Delhi, 1980).

revolts the earlier flexible relationship between peasants and the state would have changed—with the intermediate grantees playing the difficult role of keeping the peasants tied since it was not only the revenue demands of the state but also their own revenue rights which were at stake. This points towards an urgent need on the part of grantees and landowners and clan chiefs, the potential ruling families, to not only insist on their high status but to be able to prove it whenever necessary. An emphasis on status, with the insistence on service by the lower orders inherent in the formulation of *varṇa*, became in some areas an adjunct to coercion by those who had succeeded in rising to higher levels of political power. The *itihāsa-purāṇa* tradition became one of the means of legitimizing status and the *vaṁśānucarita* sections had to be carefully preserved.

Lists of succession (*vaṁśa*)—whether of teachers as in the Vedic texts, or of Elders in the *saṅgha*, or of descent groups as in the case of the Sūryavaṁśa and the Candravaṁśa, or of dynasties—encapsulate perceptions of the past. Genealogy as a record of succession lay at the core of the epic tradition and linked epic to embedded history as well as to the *itihāsa-purāṇa* and later historical forms. Genealogy is used by new groups in the ascendant to legitimize their power and claim connections with those who were earlier in power. Links were therefore sought in the post-Gupta period by new ruling families with the Sūryavaṁśa and the Candravaṁśa. The epics embodying the stories of these lineages were thus assured continuity, quite apart from the infusion of a religious dimension through the theory of epic heroes being *avatāras* of Viṣṇu. The less obvious information from genealogical data indicates kinship patterns, marriage forms, geographical settlements and migration.[31]

The pattern or structure of a genealogy is often indicative of social integration where competing groups are shown through a

[31] Romila Thapar, 'Genealogy as a source of Social History,' *AISH*, p. 326ff.

listing of descent. Among these the successful ones claim a larger share of the genealogical structure, parallel to their claim to inheritance and power. In the Aila genealogy, for example, the Pūrus and the Yādavas claim the major part of the genealogy and the lines of Turvaśa, Anu and Druhyu peter out fairly soon. The ideological function of the genealogy is to legitimate those who have succeeded to power or to subvert the claims of those who for various reasons are unacceptable. That genealogy was of considerable consequence is indicated not only by the *Purāṇa*s but also by other sources.[32]

The *vaṁśānucarita* section has three distinct constituent parts.[33] The first is the mythical section of the rule of the seven Manus, which is wiped away by the action of the Flood. This is followed by the detailed listing of the generations in each of the two major lineages. The Ikṣvāku is the senior and more cohesive. Descent is recorded only from eldest son to eldest son with a tight control over a well demarcated territory, indicative of a stronger tendency towards monarchy and primogeniture. The Aila lineage is more akin to the pattern of a segmentary system with a wide geographical distribution involving northern, western and central India. Possibly it reflects a more assimiliative system in which the segments are less the result of branching off or migrating away from the main lineage and more a record of alliances with existing clans. The spread of the Haihaya group in central India would suggest this. It might also be the result of an element of the 'tidying up' of lineages by the authors of the *Purāṇa*s. Two sub-lineages

[32] Pliny in *Natural History*, VI. 21.4–5, quotes Megathenes as stating that the Indians count 154 kings upto the time of Alexander. Genealogical data is also contained in the seals and in most land-grant inscriptions from the Gupta period onwards, e.g. Sonpat Copper Seal of Harshavardhana, in J.F. Fleet, ed., *C.I.I.*, vol. III, Inscriptions of the Early Gupta Kings (Varanasi, 1970), p. 231: Ralanpur Stone Inscription of Jajalladeva I, V.V. Mirashi, ed., *C.I.I.* vol. IV, Inscriptions of the Kalacuri-Cedi Era (Ootacamund, 1955), p. 409; the Lakhamandala inscription, *Epigraphia Indica.*, I, 1892, p. 10ff.

[33] Romila Thapar, *op. cit.*

among the Candravaṁśa are given pre-eminence, those of the Purus controlling the western Ganga valley and the more diffused Yādavas migrating to western and central India. The segments are all treated as *kṣatriyas*, even though at times this status conflicts with the status assigned to some of them in other sources.[34] Thus the genealogy was a method of legitimizing all those who had held power. However, they had to have performed the brahmanical sacrificial ritual in order to be included in the *itihāsa-purāṇa*, for those who were lax in this matter were either dropped altogether, such as the Licchavis, or like the Śākyas were merely mentioned *en passant*.[35]

The *Mahābhārata* war acts as another time-marker and brings to the battlefield virtually all the lineages of the Candravaṁśa, and a few others as well, and marks the death of the lineages. That it was a terminal event is reflected in the switch to the future tense after the war, suggesting a prophetic form, and is followed by details on dynastic succession in the kingdom of Magadha, an area which emerged in fact as the most powerful kingdom of the Ganga valley. Descent lists now become king lists mentioning historically attested dynasties—Nandas, Mauryas, Śuṅgas, Kāṇvas, Āndhras, and so on, as well as the regnal years of kings. The genealogical record thus indicates a change to monarchies during this period, a change which was of considerable historical importance. Those dynasties which did not claim links with earlier descent groups such as the Indo-Greeks, Śakas, Kuṣāṇas and Kṣatrapas receive short shrift at the hands of the genealogists. The Yavanas as a

[34] Pargiter, *The Ancient Indian Historical Tradition*, p. 109ff; *Manu*, X. 8, X. 23 refers to the Āndhras and Sātvats as *śūdras*. the Āndhras are identified with the Andhaka of the Andhaka-Vṛṣṇi group and the Vṛṣṇis married the Sātvats. Pāṇini, II.2.95 and VI.2, 34, refers to the Andhaka and the Vṛṣṇis as being *kṣatriya gotras*. The events of the *Mahābhārata* suggest that the Vṛṣṇis were of a lower status, judging by the objection of some of the *kṣatriyas* present to giving Kṛṣṇa the status of the honoured guest. Sabhāparvan, pp. 33.26ff; 34.1ff.

[35] *Viṣṇu Purāṇa*, IV. 22.

generalized term are described as the descendants of the Turvaśa, who, as a segment of the Candravaṁśa, become relatively insignificant fairly early in the genealogical listing.[36] The entry of *śūdra*s as kings, be they Indian or foreign, was of course seen as the inevitable consequence of social imbalances foretold for the Kaliyuga. The *vaṁśānucarita* section therefore becomes a preservation of the record of social and political relations as perceived at a crucial historical moment, and incorporates much of what was believed to be historically accurate. This is put together in a distinctive structure which not only gives form to the past but also becomes a charter of sanction for existing social institutions as well as a potential charter for future claims to legitimacy and status.

Purāṇic literature, in the sections other than the *vaṁśānucarita,* reflects facets of change which impinged upon the historical tradition. It comprises essentially assimilative texts where the Sanskritic tradition and the local tradition are sought to be intermeshed. This was inevitable in a situation where those of a Sanskritic cultural milieu received grants of land and settled in areas where the exposure to Sanskritic culture had been relatively sparse, if at all. Some degree of mutual interchange was required, even if for no other purpose than that of establishing dominance. The Purāṇic texts with their various sub-categories are facets of this development. The culture of the dominant and of the subordinate remained distinct, but proximity and some degree of absorption smoothened the edges of an otherwise angular relationship in many areas. The rhetoric of the Great Tradition and the systematizing of substratum cultures, both of which are reflected in the *Purāṇa*s, made the literature acceptable to the audience and useful in mobilizing social and political action.[37]

[36] *Mahābhārata,* Ādiparvan, 80.1ff.

[37] Examples of such adjustments extend even to the literal Sanskritization of non-Sanskrit names, and to the story which relates the event, e.g. the Śailodbhava dynasty in its origin myth relates the story of how a *brāhmaṇa* was requested to create a man out of chips of rock, and thus the ancestor of the Śailodbhavas was created, the story evidently explaining the Sanskriti-

V

A more clearly recognizable historical tradition is evident in the post-Gupta period, linked in part to the historical changes of the early and mid first millennium AD. The states of this period were territorially not as large as the Mauryan and the Kuṣāṇa, for example. There was a multiplicity of state formation, particularly in areas hitherto regarded as peripheral or marginal and often characterized by a lineage society. Many of these new states emerged as a consequence of the changes in agrarian relations in the earlier established states, when the system of making grants of land became current. These changes required new processes of authority, law and revenue collection in areas which earlier were either outside the state system or on the edge of it. The change was not limited to the political arena but also introduced new forms of a wider social mobility. There was a growth of sectarian religious groups, some of which professed a doctrinal cult (*bhakti*, narrowing in on an individual's devotion to a particular deity); others which attempted to systematize more earthly cults of fertility and magic; and still others which remained loyal lay supporters of the Buddhist and Jaina *saṅgha*. It was also perhaps in part a reaction to this last group which motivated the increasing interest in an *itihāsa-purāṇa*. Both the Buddhists and the Jainas had shown a sense of centring their sects in avowedly historical events which imparted a certain historicity and added to the intellectual strength of their institutions. The historicity of the Buddha and Mahāvīra was emphasized, major events in the history of the respective *saṅgha*s were linked to political events and personalities, chronology was often calculated on the basis of the date of the death of the Buddha and of Mahāvīra. This point was not missed by other groups and in the latter half of the first millennium AD when Vaiṣṇava and Śaiva sects competed for royal patronage, they not only established monastic institutions but also introduced

zation of a non-Sanskrit name. R.G. Basak, *History of North-Eastern India* (Calcutta, 1967), p. 211ff.

a historical dimension into the discussion on the evolution of the sect. It can be argued that Buddhist and Jaina sects arose as a part of a counter-culture and therefore as groups in dissent had a clearer sense of their historical purpose.[38] This is a partial explanation of a far more complex question: why Buddhism has a more recognizable sense of externalized history—a question which cannot be discussed in this brief essay. Be it said in passing that apart from considerations of eschatology and epistemology, all of which have their own significance, it is as well to consider also that Buddhism and Jainism were quite early on institutionally based and moved fairly soon to becoming property holders on a considerable scale. As such the records of their evolution did not merely narrate the life of the Buddha and the history of the *saṅgha* (with its various divergent sects, each claiming status and authenticity), but also described the building of monasteries, the amassing of property and the rights to controlling these—rights which became complex and competitive with the fissioning off of sects from the main stems. The sense of the historicity of the sect becomes evident even in Śaiva and Vaiṣṇava sects when they begin to locate themselves in *āśrama*s and *maṭha*s and become immensely wealthy property holders, and when intensified competition for patronage has to be supported by claims to legitimacy—which require a substantial input of historically phrased argument.

Implicit in the genealogical form is the notion of time and chronology. The arrangement of events in a chronological order is less precise for earlier times and only when sequential causation becomes important does chronological precision enter the focus of history. Genealogical generations indicate time periods, as also do regnal years. The latter move from fanciful figures to more credible ones as the dynastic lists approach historically attested time. Thus the chronology given for the Śiśunāga, Nandas, Mauryas and other dynasties is feasible. The arrangement of chronological

[38] Romila Thapar, 'Renunciation: the making of a Counter-culture?,' in *AISH*, p. 63ff.

order becomes more important as historical memory becomes less embedded. The cosmological time of the *mahāyuga* and the start of the Kaliyuga gives way to historical time.[39] The accuracy of historical time increases by the reference to dateable eras—the Kṛta (c. 58 BC), Śaka (AD 78), Gupta (AD 319–20), Cedi (c. AD 249), Harṣa (AD 606), and so on: and by the very precise dates recorded in era, regnal year, season, month, lunar fortnight and day in the inscriptions. The era, apart from commemorating an event, can also be seen as a capturing of time, symbolic of an articulation of power in a context where time is viewed as part of an eventual point of destruction. The word for time is *kāla* from the root *kal* 'to calculate', which suggests a meaning indicative of measurement.

[39] Cosmological time moves in the Mahāyuga of 4,320,000 years and the complete cycle is then divided into four *yugas*: the Kṛta of 1,728,000 years; the Tretā of 1,296,000 years, the Dvāpara of 864,000 years and the Kaliyuga of 432,000 years, the size of the *yugas* declining in arithmetical progression. The Kaliyuga is crucial and there is a regular reduction by substracting the length of the Kaliyuga from each preceding *yuga*, an orderliness which is basic to the concept. The numbers used are quasi-mathematical, a mixture of magic and astronomy. Numbers such as 3,7,12 and 72 are considered magical and constitute the fractions in the figures. Thus 432,000 = 60 × 7200, and this further introduces the sexagesimal unit of 60, frequently used in ancient West Asia as well as in south Indian astrology. The Babylonian tradition also uses 72,1,200 and 432,000 for its chronology (J. Campbell, *The Masks of the Gods*, vol. II, New York, 1959, p. 128ff.) and the *Jyotiṣa-vedāṅga* shows a familiarity with Babylonian astronomy and mathematics. (D. Pingree, 'The Mesopotamian Origin of Early Indian Mathematical Astronomy,' *Journal for the History of Astronomy*, 1973, IV, pp. 1–12.) The figure of 72 years is taken to calculate the processional lag moving over one degree and 432,000 is the basis of calculating the epicycle. Was cosmological time the earlier and more popular astronomical knowledge which was deliberately preserved in this manner, as distinct from the mathematics and the solar-based astronomy of the period reflected in the more formal writings of scientists of later times? As a contrast to these majuscule dimensions there are also the miniscule fractional parts of time listed in Jaina texts of the late first and the early second millennia AD. Interestingly, the description of the *yugas* and *kalpas* is spatial, e.g. *Saṁyutta Nikāya*, XV.1.5–8.

Perhaps because of the cyclical theory it was also associated with destruction in the sense of the end of time.

The inevitability of time is strengthened by the use of prophecies in genealogies, for time is the ultimate destroyer, *mahākāla*. Cosmological time is distinct from historical time not only by its mathematical pattern and the spatial form in its description, but also by its total orderliness, an orderliness which emphasizes its unreality. This in part might also explain the marginality of chiliastic and millenarian movements in such a pattern as compared to the Judaeo-Christian tradition in which they play a distinctive role. The coming of Viṣṇu as Kalkin arises out of an anxiety relating to the present—the wish to terminate the inequities of the Kaliyuga through Viṣṇu yet again being incarnated as a saviour figure. But such a termination is predetermined by the length of the cycle and will in any case lead to the ultimate ending of the cycle. It is more to the weakness of the eschatology that the marginality of millenarian movements can be attributed. The interplay of cosmological and historical time in the brahmanical tradition can perhaps be explained partially by the *yajña* and *varṇa* requirements which were part of the process of legitimizing families and cults. Cyclical time it has been argued, goes counter to an eschatology which would point to a historical change towards a directed goal.[40] Yet within the *mahāyuga* there is an emphasis on change. It is change rather than repetition which is inherent in the concept, and within this the explanation of change is also implicit.[41]

The notion of change is even more central to the Buddhist concept of time.[42] Because of the claim to the historicity of the Buddha there is a single, central point to which all events relate chronologically, namely the Mahāparinirvāṇa, the death of the

[40] M. Eliade, *Cosmos and History* (New York, 1959).
[41] Kalhaṇa, *Rājataraṅginī*, V. 21.
[42] A.L. Basham, *The Wonder That Was India* (London, 1964), pp. 272–3; *Dīgha Nikāya*, III, p. 75ff.

Buddha. Buddhist eschatology envisages the extinction of consciousness in *nirvāna*, which, although seemingly negative, is the aim of human endeavour since it is a release from rebirth. Change within cosmological time is emphasized further by the cyclic movement of time taking the form of a spiral, in that the cycle never returns to its point of origin: and a spiral if fully stretched can become a wave, if not a linear form. The rise and fall within the cycle purports constant change and even the fall carries within it the eventual upward swing of the cycle, and this is conducive to the idea of a coming millennium, an idea envisaged in the Buddha Maitreya. This in turn is paralleled by decay carrying within it the seeds of regeneration.

The precision of historical time as recorded in inscriptions probably derived from the more widespread use of the solar calendar from the first millennium AD. But it also had to do with the legitimacy of the individual in authority, for the inscription was frequently a legal charter. Not only was the authority of the king time bound in such charters, but so also was his claim to the property which he was donating in as much as later kings could revoke these grants in spite of the insistence in the inscriptions that they were given in perpetuity. An additional factor was the influence of the idea that all actions are conditioned by the auspiciousness of the moment when they are carried out, and in the case of donations and grants this would be particularly apposite.[43] The multiple use of historical time focused on the individual and gave

[43] Some of the dates for inscriptions were provided by astrologers, and these include astronomical details. However they are not always correct. D.C. Sircar, *Studies in Society and Administration of Ancient and Medieval India*, vol. I (Calcutta, 1967), pp. 171–2. It is worth noting that apart from the legal charters, another sphere of life in which time was very precisely recorded was the horoscope. As a corollary to this it is interesting that an almost exact counterpart to the careful record of time in inscriptions is to be found in discussions on the precise time for conducting a *yajña*, where the time is again indicated in terms of the year, season, month, lunar fortnight, constellation, date and time of day.

sharper definition to the individual as a figure of authority: an idea by no means unfamiliar by now in the historical consciousness of the period. A fuller exposition of this idea had come from Buddhist sources. Aśoka Maurya, as a patron of Buddhism, acquired an accretion of legends, some of which were gathered into the *Aśokāvadāna*. The attempt was to give historicity to the Buddhist *saṅgha* by linking it to a powerful political personality, a notion which was not alien to the emergence of much of the other non-Buddhist *carita* literature. The need to write the biography of the Buddha, *buddha-carita,* had been felt since the time of the early monastic movement and the first missions. It changed from being a part of the canonical texts to a separate genre of literature.[44] Gradually the idea of biography was extended to the 'hero' in a wider context. A historical background is also helpful to organized missionary activity in new areas where antecedents have to be explained; this was useful to the entry of Buddhism into Asia, as indeed it was useful to brahmanical centres in the more remote parts of the Indian subcontinent. The *carita* tradition doubtless also drew on the *praśasti*s incorporated in a number of early inscriptions, such as that of Khāravela at Hāthigumphā and Rudradāman at Junagadh; a style which became more elaborate in time as evidenced by the Udaipur *rāj-praśasti.*[45]

VI

Those in authority seek validation from the past, and this validation was the starting point of a new category of texts, the *vaṁśāvalī*s and the *caritas* of the post-Gupta period. The *vaṁśāvalī*s were the histories of the ruling families in specific geographical regions, the latter often coinciding with the new kingdoms and states in

[44] This change is reflected in the difference between the *Suttas* and the *Vinaya,* where the life of the Buddha is part of canonical scripture, and Aśvaghoṣa's *Buddhacarita,* which is a biography *per se.*

[45] D.C. Sircar, *Select Inscriptions,* second edition (Calcutta, 1965), pp. 213–19, 175–80; *Epigraphia Indica,* vol. XXIX, 1951–2, parts 1–5, pp. 1–90.

areas previously either unoccupied or settled by groups of tribes. As a genre they lay between the lineage lists of the *Purāṇas* and the historical biographies of individual rulers. The *carita* or historical biography was a complement to the *vaṁśāvalī* and focused on the king, who was seen as the centre of authority in a more radial state system. Bāṇabhaṭṭa's *Harṣacarita* led off the biographical form and was followed by a large number of others.[46] Most of the better known ones were written between the eighth and twelfth centuries AD, but as a form *carita* literature continued into later times, in each case commemorating the rise of new kings. The *carita* was unashamedly the eulogy of the patron, but the persons chosen were those who had a special status and function in the ruling family and were contributors of a more than ordinary kind, not only to their own families but also to the consolidation of kingdoms and kingship. The rhetoric of eulogy when deconstructed would doubtless reveal multiple relationships within a courtly edifice of norms and actions, and despite the ambiguity in presenting hard historical data much of the subtlety of historical nuance can be gathered from these biographies. *Carita* literature also focuses on other aspects of the individual in society. Cyclic time carries a certain inevitability but the individual can opt out of it, and on a lesser level this is demonstrated in biographies where the *karma* of the individual may play a larger role than the inevitability of the time cycle: and the individual *karma* and its historic role was central to the doctrine of Buddhism as well as the ideology of the *bhakti* tradition.

On occasion the subjects of the biographies were younger brothers who had come to rule (as for example, Harṣavardhana and Vikramāditya VI), and their legitimacy over other claimants

[46] Such as Vākapati's *Gauḍavāho* on Yaśovarman of Kannauj; Bilhaṇa's *Vikramānkadevacarita* on Vikramāditya VI, the Cālukya king; Sandhyākaranandin's *Rāmacarita* on Rāmapāla; Jayānaka's *Pṛthvīrājavijaya*; Nayacandra Sūri's *Hammīra-mahākāvya*; Someśvaradeva's *Kīrtikaumudi*, a biography of Vastupāla, who, although not a king, was a person of great political importance; and Hemacandra's *Kumārapālacarita*.

had to be established. The royal patron was linked with the major lineages of the *itihāsa-purāṇa* or with a new lineage which had acquired status since then, such as the Agni-kula among Rajputs or the Nāgavaṁśa among certain central Indian dynasties. The *carita* was essentially a literary form in origin and thus a far cry from the bardic fragments of epic times. The most sophisticated courtly tradition found expression in this literature and the courtly values of chivalry, heroism and loyalty were at a premium.[47] Two obvious characteristics of this form were the depiction of the king as the focus of the court and a clear awareness of a well-defined geographical area which constituted the kingdom and was identified with the dynasty. Obeisance is made to the lineage but it plays a secondary role in relation to the king who is now most clearly the figure of formal political authority in both state and society.

Political decentralization inherent in the granting of land on a large scale encouraged a competition among families aspiring to dynastic status. Dynasties survived through an assertion of power, legitimacy and recourse to marriage alliances with ambitious feudatories. Attempts to restructure the economic potential within certain areas of the state and to balance the intricate relationship between royal power, brahmanical authority and the dominant religious cults of the region become a further support to power. The emphasis on territory had again to do with the jostling of new states and with the legitimizing of the economic and administrative changes which the system of land grants introduced into the kingdoms.

The *vaṁśāvalī* was the chronicle of a dynasty, and inevitably also the chronicle of the territory controlled by the dynasty. The *vaṁśāvalī* therefore used as source material the various local *Purāṇa*s as well as the oral tradition.[48] It became the characteristic

[47] V.S. Pathak, *Ancient Historians of India* (Bombay, 1966), p. 21ff.

[48] The sources drawn upon by the authors of the *vaṁśāvalī*s included the *sthala-purāṇa*s, *upa-purāṇa*s, *tīrtha-purāṇa*s, caste *purāṇa*s and *mahātmyas*, all of

literature of the new states in various parts of the subcontinent in the early second millennium AD. This is indicative of some elements of similarity in historical change, which in turn reflects a degree of cultural uniformity. These elements do not indicate the influence of one dominant regional culture over the others, but rather the expression of a similar historical situation, which, formulated in a certain kind of literature, was common to many regions.

The structure of the *vaṁśāvalī* was almost identical in all these regions. The earliest section narrated the origin myths pertaining to the region and the dynasty. In this there was a recording of local lore as well as a borrowing from the *itihāsa-purāṇa* tradition. Attempts were made to link local history with themes from the

---

which were texts recording the past and the evolution of places, sects and deities, locations of pilgrimage, dominant castes and local history. Such texts were part of the larger Purāṇic tradition and, although conforming to the major *Purāṇa*s in sprit if not in form, included a large amount of local and regional data. The oral sources consisted of bardic fragments and ballads on local heroes and events of significance, not to mention the genealogies and marriage alliances of land-owning families, for the bardic tradition was still alive, as it remains to this day. It has been argued that Kalhaṇa's *Rājataraṅginī*, a fine example of a *vaṁśāvalī*, was a unique document in that it was the only genuine piece of historical writing from India (A.L. Basham, 'The Kashmir Chronicle,' in C.H. Philips, *Historians of India, Pakistan and Ceylon* (Oxford, 1961), p. 57ff). Yet the *vaṁśāvalī* form occurs in various parts of the country—from the neighbouring Chamba *vaṁśāvalī* (Ph. Vogel, *The Antiquities of Chamba State*, Calcutta, 1911, *A.S.I.*, vol. 36) to the most distant *Mūṣakavaṁśa* or chronicle of the Ay dynasty in Kerala. Gopinath Rao, 'Extracts from the Mūṣakavaṁśam . . . ,' *Travancore Archaeological Series*, 1916, II.1, no. 10, pp. 87–113; See also M.G.S. Narayanan, 'History from Muśaka-vaṁśa-kāvya of Atula,' *P.A.I.O.C.* (Jadhavpur, 1969). Curiously in both cases the founder is born in a cave (*guhā*) and is associated with a *mūṣaka-vaṁśa* (literally: 'mouse lineage'). A better known cave association is of course that of the Guhilots of Mewar (J. Tod, I, p. 173ff.). For further lists of *vaṁśāvalī*s see A.K. Warder, *Introducfion to Indian Historiography* (Bombay, 1972), and J.P. de Souza and C.M. Kulkarni, eds., *Historiography in Indian Languages* (Delhi, 1972).

Purāṇas incorporating the myths and the genealogies of the Great Tradition with local persons and places. The *Purāṇas* were the prototypes and local personalities were the protagonists. This required the continued availability of the *Purāṇas* as sources from which the *vaṁśāvalīs* could draw. The major part of the text, however, dealt with more contemporary events, and a history of the ruling dynasty was narrated giving its genealogy and referring to important events associated with the dynasty. The veracity of this information can often be ascertained by comparing it with the evidence of inscriptions, since many of the grants of land were recorded on copper plates or on temple walls. Whereas the need for a *vaṁśāvalī* was motivated by the acquisition of power, the historically authenticated section would appear to coincide with the constitution of power, often articulated in the taking of royal titles such as *mahārājādhirāja*. Concomitant with this was the acceptance of responsibilities of power by the family. The authors of the *vaṁśāvalīs* were court poets and officials and were therefore familiar with political and administrative concerns. The *vaṁśāvalīs* would also be important to those who received grants of land in vouching for the legitimacy of the granting authority.

The *vaṁśāvalī* differs from the earlier tradition in that it legitimates a particular family and not an entire lineage, and to that extent the legitimation of lineage is indirect. The family was not seen merely as a household of agnatic and affinal kinsfolk but was the hub of power. It drew its strength both from claims to high descent as well as to property. Marriage alliances were controlled because dowry and inheritance were a part of the property structure. Such forms of the legitimation of families in power and of regions was of more immediate necessity to newly risen families in small states. The *vaṁśāvalī* therefore was by its very nature not a record of expansionist states. The major dynasties of the past, such as the Nandas and Mauryas, were not the models and only the very early lineages were considered possible sources of status. The appeal was not to the political system of the state but to sources of power which could back up the economic reality of aristocratic families with visions of dynastic ambition. It is significant that the *caritas* and the *vaṁśāvalīs* take up the narrative, as it were, from where the major *Purāṇas* leave off. The Purāṇic accounts of the ruling dynasties come to a close soon after the Guptas. The dynasties listed prior to these are mainly of the core regions of the Ganga valley and western and northern India. That the account was not continued in these *Purāṇas* was probably because there was a bigger distribution of centres of power in the post-Gupta period, and in each of such areas local *Purāṇas* and chronicles of various kinds began to be maintained. These texts often incorporate both the Purāṇic tradition and the local tradition, as is exemplified in those cases where legitimation is sought by reference to local myths of descent—as in the case of the Agni-kula Rajputs and the Nagavaṁśis of central India.

As a form the *vaṁśāvalī* was not restricted to dynastic chronicles and was adapted to the history of other institutions as well. Some of these were monastic institutions where not only was the succession of elders chronicled but also their relations with political authority. This dynastic and political information pertained either to royal patrons of the institution or recorded relations between the institution and political authority, generally in the context of the institution establishing its own legitimacy. An early expression of this relationship is evident from the Buddhist tradition where monastic chronicles were a regular part of the historical tradition.[49]

[49] The *Mahāvaṁsa*, as the chronicle of the Mahāvihāra monastery in Sri Lanka composed in the mid first millennium AD, is primarily concerned with establishing its legitimacy both as the fount of the pristine teaching of the Buddha as well as in its interaction with political authority. Thus the Theravāda sect, which was established in the Mahāvihāra monastery, is said to have originated from the schism at the Council of Pāṭaliputra, called at the initiative of Aśoka Maurya, and was established in Sri Lanka largely through the patronage of Devānampiya Tissa. Buddhist chronicles do tend to show a greater degree of historical determinism. Sri Lanka is predestined for the establishment of Buddhism. Events move towards proclaiming the

In attempting to establish the legitimacy of the dynasties or institutions whose history they are recording, chronicles stress the uniqueness of historical events relating to the origin and history of the subject of the chronicle, with indications of its growth and change. Actions are directed towards a goal, often resulting in the success of the subject. Chronicles are therefore compiled when a dynasty or institution has established itself and is recognized as powerful. The chronicle helps to establish its claims to authority over competing groups, especially those which are politically important. The borrowing from the *itihāsa-purāṇa* tradition suggests continuity and also stresses legitimacy, for the new group is seen as being related to those who were in power in the past and can also claim antiquity by maintaining these connections with earlier lineages. The chronicle is again the statement of the successful group and manages to deflect if not erase the presence of competitors. This becomes a particularly useful aspect of the chronicle in a society where not only dissent but even protest often takes the form of opting out or migration away, in preference to confrontation.[50]

If changing forms in the expression of historical consciousness symbolize historical change, and if changes in the political forms of society are reflected in the nature of historical expression, then the *itihāsa-purāṇa* tradition would point to three phases in the unfolding of early Indian history. Initially, in lineage societies, historical consciousness was embedded and recorded the perception of the ordering of lineages. With the evolution of states in northern India the second phase was inaugurated, focusing on dynastic power and the supremacy of the state as a system which in the political arena seems to have overridden caste ordering. The

primacy of the *saṅgha*. L.S. Perera, 'The Pali Chronicles of Ceylon,' in C.H. Philips. p. 29ff. This is further emphasized by the notion of causality and contract so central to Buddhist ethics, and by the historical role of the missionaries who propagate Buddhism in new areas.

[50] Romila Thapar, 'Dissent and Protest in the Early Indian Tradition,' *Studies in History*, 1979, vol. I, no. 2, pp. 177–95.

post-Gupta period saw a change in the structure of the state, accompanied by the need in many cases for the legitimation of status of ruling families.

Historical consciousness in early India took a form which grew out of embedded history. Part of the explanation for this may lie in the fact that the *varṇa* ordering of society, which never fully coincided with a clearly defined socio-economic stratification, carried a large element of the lineage-based structure and therefore also the embedded history of that structure. Where *kṣatriya* legitimation became necessary, the *itihāsa-purāṇa* tradition was strengthened with a drawing upon embedded history for origins. In such cases the past in relation to political power became a *kṣatriya* past. But at the same time it did not remain embedded. Although the origin myths of the dynasties recorded in the *vaṁśāvalīs* become something of a *mantra* or a formula, this should not hide the fact that despite the continuing idiom from the past there is a substantial historical core in the *vaṁśāvalī* which is distinguished from the embedded section, and which is therefore a break from the past and takes the form of historical consciousness expressed as externalized history.

Index